Sold!

Books that make you better

Books that make you better. That make you *be* better, *do* better, *feel* better. Whether you want to upgrade your personal skills or change your job, whether you want to improve your managerial style, become a more powerful communicator, or be stimulated and inspired as you work.

Prentice Hall Business is leading the field with a new breed of skills, careers and development books. Books that are a cut above the mainstream – in topic, content and delivery – with an edge and verve that will make you better, with less effort.

Books that are as sharp and smart as you are.

Prentice Hall Business.
We work harder – so you don't have to.

For more details on products, and to contact us, visit
www.pearsoned.co.uk
www.yourmomentum.com

STEVE MARTIN AND GARY COLLERAN

Sold!

How to make it easy for people
to buy from you

London • New York • Toronto • Sydney • Tokyo • Singapore
Hong Kong • Cape Town • Madrid • Paris • Amsterdam • Munich • Milan

PEARSON EDUCATION LIMITED

Head Office:
Edinburgh Gate
Harlow CM20 2JE
Tel: +44 (0)1279 623623
Fax: +44 (0)1279 431059
www.pearsoned.co.uk

First published in Great Britain 2003

ISBN 0 273 67518 4

British Library Cataloguing in Publication Data
A CIP catalogue record for this book can be obtained from the British Library.

10 9 8 7 6 5 4 3 2

Designed by Claire Brodmann Book Designs, Lichfield, Staffs
Typeset by Northern Phototypesetting Co. Ltd, Bolton
Printed and bound in Great Britain by Bell & Bain Ltd, Glasgow

The Publishers' policy is to use paper manufactured from sustainable forests.

Dedications

To the memory of John Martin
16 June 1939–18 February 2000
(Steve's dad)

To Irene
(Gary's mum)

... And to Colin

'Can both my customer and I
smile about the time we
spent together?'

How often can we answer
'absolutely yes' to this question?

Contents

Acknowledgements   ix

Introduction   xi

Chapter 1
Creating and maintaining a valuable customer relationship
(Liking and listening)   1

Chapter 2
Establishing what is valuable to the customer
(Being productive)   23

Chapter 3
Providing what is valuable to the customer
(Giving 'em what they want)   49

Chapter 4
Gaining a commitment to action
(Sold!)   63

Chapter 5
Creating a well-formed sales goal
(Getting ready)   77

Chapter 6
Sold!
(Effective selling in action)   95

Acknowledgements

A book can often say as much about the people who influence the authors as the authors themselves. There is no doubt that *Sold!* has been born as much from the amazing people we have had the honour and pleasure to work and play with over the years including work colleagues, business partners and the clients of Sales interAction, our training company. To each and every one of you we extend a genuine thank you. We are better people for knowing you all.

We are indebted to our loved ones, families and friends for their love, support and guidance. We know that we can both be occasional pains in the arse, so thank you for bearing and being with us.

We would also like to recognize some of the individuals who are the true heroes and heroines of *Sold!* To Ed Percival, for seeing that we were on to something and then devoting time and energy to convincing us of the same. To the Effective Selling Programme distribution team and the great people who run the ESP training workshops.

We owe a huge debt to Professor Robert Cialdini whose book *Influence – Science and Practice* (Allyn and Bacon) and research into social influence has provided us with clear and practical applications to give sales people the competitive edge. And to Bobette Gordon, who is without doubt one of the most vivacious and entertaining people we have ever met.

To everyone at Phoenix, our creative and marketing agency, and to John Landers for providing the book's sketches and cartoons – thank you.

Finally we would like to thank two very special people, without whom we would still be in the pub talking about how cool it would be to write a book and not, as is the case at the time of writing these acknowledgements, in the pub toasting it. Anne Buckingham has played a huge part in every single word we have written and Rachael Stock, our editor at Prentice Hall Business, has provided her untiring input and guidance throughout. We really appreciate all your help and support. You are two incredible women and if you were with us now we'd buy you both a drink.

Cheers!

Steve & Gary

**Creating a well-formed
sales goal**
Get ready!

**Gaining a
commitment
to action**
Sold!

Effective
selling
programme

**Creating and
maintaining a
valuable
customer
relationship**
Liking and
listening

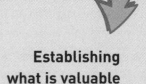

**Providing
what
is valuable to
the customer**
Giving 'em what they want

**Establishing
what is valuable
to the customer**
Being productive

Introduction

AAAAGH! CUSTOMERS

Don't they understand that people in sales have a job to do? Don't they understand that you're trying to do your best by them? You try your damnedest day in and day out to provide them with the best service and the best advice and all they seem to be interested in is how much it is going to cost. Sometimes they're not interested at all, they just pretend to be; and other times they're just coming to you because they want to find out how your product is better than a competitor's so they can try to play one off against the other.

Don't get me wrong, I don't mean that they are all like that. A lot of customers are really nice. They are a joy to do business with. They listen to what you have to say, they take on board your ideas, they even pay on time. But for every customer like that, you can generally think of three or four who are rude, difficult to deal with and treat you as if you were something that they just stepped in on the street. Don't they understand that you have a job to do? Don't they understand that if they gave you a few moments of their time you might be able to do something valuable and worthwhile for them? If only they would put themselves in your position for a few moments, understand the pressures that you are under from the company you work for. Every day seems to get busier and busier and you work with a company that demands sales growth every single month, every single quarter and every single year. It's a challenging time. I quite like a challenge but the fact of the matter is that there's something that gets in the way of you achieving the challenges and the goals that you're set. It's the bloody customer again. If only you could have more of those nice, polite, interested customers, the ones who like doing business with you.

Imagine what that would be like. Imagine a group of customers that buy stuff when you have got stuff to sell them. Imagine that they just don't argue about the price, they just ask where to send the cash or the cheque or just give you their credit card without even thinking. Imagine what it would be like if they let you choose the products or the service that was best for them. Imagine if every one of them thought that, genuinely, you were on their side. Imagine what it would be like if they just came back time and time again to you – yeah, that would be good!

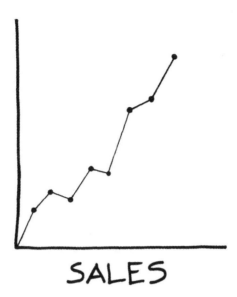

SALES

AAAAGH! SALES PEOPLE

If indeed that's what they call themselves. There are so many different names for them: customer service agent, account manager, customer information specialists, it's all so confusing. Surely they're all there just to sell to me, aren't they? Actually, some of them even pretend not to be sales people. I've lost count of the number of times I've sat down in the evening and the telephone rings. 'Good evening' they say, . . . 'my name is . . . such and such from . . . such and such company. I am just conducting some sort of consumer survey, would it be OK if I asked you a few questions, I promise that I'm not selling you anything'. It doesn't have to happen too many times before I'm suspicious of everyone that calls me.

It happens in the shops too, when I'm out and about and even when I'm at work. Sales people trying to be nice, giving their false smiles and attempting to appear as my friend, they are not my friends. Worst of all is when they totally ignore me. When I'm in a queue in a garage or in a store, some of them don't even recognise I'm there, sometimes I feel that I'm interrupting them, even though it's me who's handing over the money.

The fact is, I don't really have anything against sales people. In fact I have been delighted with some of the interactions I have had with some sales people. But I remember the bad experiences too! I recognize that they have an important job and have to deliver what their companies ask them to, I just wish that sometimes they could try and do things a little differently. I wish that they would recognize me not only as a customer but also as an individual. I wish that they would help me to buy and advise me when I'm ready, rather than what can sometimes feel like having products forced down my throat. I also wish that some of them would take notice of me and come and help me when I look like I need some help rather than just ignore me. There is a balance here and the sales people that get it right are a joy to do business with. And when I find those kind of sales people I build a relationship with them and as a result I tend to go back to them time and again when I need something, be it a product or a service. I go back to the sales people that recognize and treat me as an individual and at the same time provide some sort of help. Yeah, if only they were all like that! Those are the sales people that make it easy for me to buy from them.

UH-OH, look out, here it comes, another book on sales! Surely there are enough out there already? Dozens of them, actually hundreds of them! We searched on Amazon.co.uk and lost count after 150 or so. A hundred and fifty or so sales books out there and each and every one promising new ways, new techniques, new ideas which will enable you to sell more to new customers, attract new customers, persuade more people more of the time. Each and every one of these publications in its own way is looking to deliver the Holy Grail in terms of successful selling. But if you think about it, it's no surprise there are so many publications, magazines, articles and books.

Customers change every day. The competition changes every day. New products; new services; new ideas; new ways of advertising and communicating with consumers and customers. The world is changing. Products and services develop a pace. There are products and services available today that you could only have dreamt of maybe just five or ten years ago. In another five or ten years the products that are available to you today will seem outdated, old fashioned, no use to you anymore. With these advances in products and services that are now available comes an increased demand on the consumer and the customer. The customers and consumers of today are more knowledgeable and more demanding, more decisive and explicit about what they want and what they need. Their lives are busier, they are exposed to more advertising, more people trying to sell their products, services and ideas.

With all these advances in information and technology, how come it's often so difficult to sell to these customers? Well, the fact is, not only have our lives and the products and services that surround our everyday lives become more complicated and complex, the business of selling those products and services and ideas has also become too complicated and complex. Why can't the job of selling be something that is straightforward and simple? It seems to have got lost in all the clutter: customer information systems; electronic customer management systems and computer programmes; very clever and technically advanced advertisements; specific and heavily targeted mailings, right down to those annoying little pop-up screens on the internet. Our ever-changing and fast-moving world has created many innovative and creative and technologically advanced ways of selling to customers. Yet one important element seems to have been lost in the whole of this process – the people themselves, the people that buy the product and service and the people that help them buy the product or service. The customers and sales people.

What's different about *Sold!* is that we are not going to promise you the Holy Grail of selling. Many of the principles and ideas in this book will not be new to an experienced sales professional. What *Sold!* is going to do though, is take away the clutter and the complexity of selling. Therefore, throughout this book we're not going to be offering you techniques to make it possible for you to sell more to customers. Instead we are going to be taking things away. Rather than giving you 30 or 40 different techniques for finding out what's important to a customer, we're going to be concentrating on the two things that you should always do. We are here to make selling simple and easy again. So rather than concentrate on new techniques, we're going to be concentrating on the essentials. But before we get into those essentials of selling, let's put things into perspective. Why is the job you do working in sales and selling so important? Well, imagine, for a few moments what the world would be like without sales people.

Imagine that every time a customer contacted a company or perhaps went into a shop, there were no sales people to advise them, if businesses just left a customer to their own devices in the hope that they would buy a product or two from them. Now imagine what it would be like if your company had no one to sell your company's products and services to. How successful would your company be?

Sales performance is the lifeblood of every business. If you think about it almost everyone is in the business of selling something. Whether you are the chief executive of a large company, an account manager, a field sales representative, a customer services agent or one of many other roles in your business, one of your key goals is to sell your products, services and ideas to a customer or consumer.

We believe that the sales person should be regarded as a professional person, someone who seeks to develop valuable relationships and help their customers and consumers to get what they want, while at the same time delivering the business goals that their company needs to thrive in a competitive environment.

The essence of this book and the principles of the Effective Selling Programme that it describes is that a sales person is employed to sell. The most successful sales people are the ones who are proud to be sales people and that success is a result of the way they create and maintain valuable working relationships with their customers that benefit everyone. *Sold!* is based on a set of principles that have been developed to give a sales person the skills and tools they need to achieve their sales goals. Our goal is to ensure that you get something of real value by reading *Sold!* – something that leads to greater successes for you, your company and your customers.

In order to achieve that goal we will be describing the essential principles that we recommend you concentrate on and put into practice while you are selling to a customer – or, as we prefer to put it when you are 'helping a customer to buy from you'. We call these principles the Effective Selling Principles. There are five of them and they are:

1 Creating a well-formed sales goal, or what we also refer to as *'Getting ready'*

2 Creating and maintaining a valuable customer relationship, or *'Liking and Listening'*

3 Establishing what is valuable to the customer, or *'Being productive'*

4 Providing what is valuable to the customer, or *'Giving 'em what they want'*

5 Gaining a commitment to action, or *'Sold!'*

We will take each of these principles in turn starting with, what might seem strange at first, the second principle. There is a good reason for this. By considering how you will use the 'customer facing' priinciples you will effectively create a well-formed sales goal anyway. It is our intention not to make things any more complicated than they need to be. When discussing each principle we will be directing your attention to often just one or two things that you will make you more effective in helping to make it easier for your customers to buy from you. The principles we will be talking to you about are founded on what actually works in practice. We will not be offering you lots and lots of different ideas for you to randomly choose from. Instead we will be giving you the straightforward set of principles that, once mastered, will make the job of selling easy for you and the job of buying easy for your customer.

But before we do talk about the Effective Selling Principles it's important that we point out early on that there are a number of prerequisites that you, as sales people, need to have already dealt with before you sell to a customer. Each of these prerequisites is worthy of mention because they are what we would call 'foundations' to your success as sales people. These 'foundations' could, in their own right, each be worthy of having a chapter devoted to them but as it is our intention to present a straightforward and uncomplicated approach to effective selling, we are going to cover them succinctly in this introduction. They are:

- **Knowledge** – the need to have sound base of knowledge related to your products, services, competitors and the marketplace in which you sell.
- **Product and self-belief** – your belief that the products and services you sell are actually good products, ones that you yourself would own or use and that you also believe in your own ability to be a successful sales person.
- **The right customer** – the fact that you are selling to the right customer, one who can make a decision about your products and services and who has the need and the resources to buy them.

Let's explore these in a little more detail.

Knowledge

More and more people have more and more access to a host of almost limitless information on a daily basis and this trend is very likely set to continue. The internet allows anyone with a computer and a phone line to search for and access information on any subject that you care to imagine.

One of our good friends is a general practitioner. We met with him recently and he told us that he could recall a time when his patients would visit him in his surgery and describe their ailments in the hope that he would be able to diagnose their problem and provide a suitable treatment. He went on to talk about the increasing number of his patients that now come into his surgery not only having researched their symptoms on the internet but who had diagnosed their disease and had even a printed list of recommended treatments. What has this to do with the importance of knowledge and dealing with customers?

Well, like our doctor friend's patients, customers these days are more likely to be better informed and more knowledgeable about not only what they want and need but also about the potential options and solutions that would fulfill those wants and needs. The options and solutions are out there for them to research themselves and in many cases they can even decide in the comfort of their own home or office what they will order and buy.

So surely this ability to access information and resources at the click of a button will make life easier for people working in the sales environment? Surely the fact that customers and potential customers have more access to greater levels of information and knowledge than ever before makes the life of the sales person or adviser easier? After all, if the customer has access to all this product information it simplifies the task of the sales person because they no longer have to digest mountains of product and service information manuals. Why bother spending time and effort learning information that is available equally easily to the customer, also at the click of a button? Surely it would be more productive and commercially viable selling to customers rather than spending the time creating or maintaining a base of knowledge?

In order to answer this point let's examine two specific points.

Firstly, having a high degree of knowledge not only about your products and services but also those of your competitors changes the perception a customer has of you. This knowledge actually builds authority and credibility. People who have authority and credibility have been proven to be more influential than those who either don't have or have low levels of credibility and authority. High levels of knowledge can also change the way a sales person behaves. People who take the time to keep continuously updated in their field of work appear more confident and believable when they talk to their customers. They communicate with an air of confidence and conviction. Another interesting point about highly knowledgeable people is that they generally don't act like experts. They don't talk down to customers and they certainly would never tell their customers how clever they are. They demonstrate their expertise when their customers ask *them* questions. These sales people are also the ones who will tend to be approached or asked first when their customers have queries or questions that they want answers to.

The second point concerns the accessibility of information that we have already referred to. The fact that there is a plethora of information available for your company's products and services means that the same level and amount exists for every other product and service available. Now think as a customer for a few moments. The fact that all this information exists and is readily accessible potentially means that a customer could spend all their free time reviewing and consuming more and more information.

Complexity and information overload at play again.

Faced with an overload of information, often much of it conflicting, what is a customer or potential customer to do? Often the simplest and easiest solution is to consult with a person they trust – a person who has given them good advice and accurate information in the past. A sales person or company representative who has taken the time to understand and get to know about their product, their competitors and the market in which they work. And that's not all. This person doesn't just do this once. They take responsibility for updating themselves on a regular basis – after all, in our fast-moving and ever-changing world things change quickly.

Like untended plants in a garden, knowledge can often get brown and smelly at the edges.

Knowledge is often akin to gardening. Like untended plants in a garden, knowledge can often get brown and smelly at the edges. Good sales people know this and have a plan to be able to regularly weed out what is no longer useful information and prepare the ground for learning new information and ideas.

Clearly, to be successful you need a way of keeping your knowledge up to date and there are some very straightforward things you can do to help yourself. You can look out in journals and trade presses for articles related to your products and the marketplace you work in. Most trades and industries have journals and periodicals of this kind. It's also valuable to share this information with customers, particularly those who don't have the time to review journals for themselves. The internet is a great source of information, and many companies have their own intranet sites to help staff keep up to date with the latest product information. Whilst there are many sources of information the desire to keep up to date and knowledgeable lies with the individual themselves. There is a maxim that is as true for knowledge as it is for gardening:

What we feed grows, what we starve dies.

Product and self-belief

Belief in what you are doing is the single most important key success factor. Research has found that a key factor that influenced sales outcomes was the fact that the sales people believed in the company they worked for, the products they were selling, had confidence in themselves and enjoyed their job. What the sales person said to the customer, how they said it, and how they presented it, all indicated personal belief in what they were doing.

A chap called Kristone once said:

If you think you are beaten, you are.

If you think you dare not, you don't.

If you'd like to win, but think you can't, it is almost certain you won't.

Life's battles don't always go to the stronger or faster person – sooner or later the person who wins is the person who thinks they can.

If you 'will' yourself to achieve your sales goals, then you can succeed. Let yourself be influenced by what you can do. Visualize your success. A positive mental attitude will reinforce belief and can help you to look at what you can achieve. There are examples of people, in many walks of life, with positive mental attitudes and they are all winners.

How often have you seen batsmen slapping their bats against one another when one of them has hit a four or a six, or a tennis player telling themselves that they can hit that ace? They focus on their strengths and remain positive. Similarly, by having a positive mental attitude those sales seem all the more achievable.

The 'right' customer

What do we mean by selling to the 'right' customer? Well, the fact is that there are some customers who are going to be more likely to buy from you than others depending on which one of three specific 'disciplines' your company falls into.

By understanding the type of discipline your company follows (or not) you'll immediately be able to ensure that the customers you sell to are the kind who are more likely to buy from you.

It's generally accepted that there are only three types of company – Price Leaders, Product Leaders and Service Leaders. While it's accepted that, in order to be successful, a company must clearly have a product of a certain standard accompanied by a level of service and a competitive price, the most successful companies tend to be those who focus on being the leader of one of the three disciplines of Product, Service and Price and then maintaining acceptable levels of the other two.

Price Leading Companies

Price Leading Companies are ones that concentrate on providing a product or service to their customers at the best (i.e. lowest) possible price. Everything about the way they do business is geared to and focused on being able to deliver the lowest possible price to the end user or customer. The customers who buy from Price Leading Companies understand that in order to get the lowest possible price they will often have to do without certain extras or luxuries. Let's give you a few examples from some well-known Price Leading Companies.

easyJet, RyanAir, SouthWest Airlines and the ever-increasing number of low-cost airlines are all examples of Price Leading Companies. They all strive to deliver to their customers the lowest possible prices for air travel. Their customers expect the lowest prices and are prepared to do without certain luxuries that would be considered normal for a customer who travels with an airline that doesn't operate in the low-cost category. As a result when you travel on these low-cost airlines you'll probably not be given drinks, refreshments or a meal on board. These are often considered luxuries that you'll have to pay extra for. Similarly the airlines won't print boarding passes or tickets (these are an unnecessary expense that will need to be passed on to the customer) in an attempt to keep costs to a minimum.

Lidl, CostCo, Argos, Comet and a number of other retailers are also good examples of Price Leading Companies. Again they strive to deliver their products and services to customers at the lowest possible prices. Also, and in a similar vein to the low-cost airlines, they make sure that their overheads and trading costs are kept to a minimum so that they can indeed deliver on their low-cost promise. Their stores could well be functional and easy to maintain. Products will be piled high in the stores to keep storage costs to a minimum and often a customer will have to pay for delivery and extras that other stores might consider to be part of the overall service they offer.

Often Price Leading Companies thrive in commodity style environments where one product or service is seen as either the same, or very similar, to all the rest available. In this situation a typical customer will quite knowingly purchase from the company that offers the lowest possible price. However, that is not always the case. Let's look at the second discipline . . .

Product Leading Companies

The Product Leading Company is different to the Price Leading Company because its focus is on delivering the best, most technologically advanced, product on the market to its customers. Product Leading Companies stop at nothing to produce the next 'must have' consumer product. They invest heavily in research and development to produce the world's best products and their customers are the sorts of people who want to own the latest and most fashionable products. The true Product Leading Company not only strives to develop the best product, it also strives to be considered as the best and the only way to do that is by continuing to outperform itself. For example, Nike, as the world's leading sports footwear and apparel company, knows that it needs to continue to produce products that are better and an improvement on its current range. Similarly the only company that Intel will ever allow to produce a computer processor that is faster, more capable and more technologically advanced than their current model is Intel itself. Let's take a few more examples and look at the influence that Product Leading Companies have on the types of customer they attract.

We've already mentioned Nike and Intel as Product Leading Companies and to this list we could add the likes of Sony, Nokia, Vodafone and perhaps British Airways.[1] These companies are primarily focused on giving their customers the best product and those customers, in return for this increased product performance, accept that they'll pay a premium. Product Leading Companies will often invest resources in the way their products and services are presented to ensure that they reach the customer in the best possible fashion. The customer is happy to purchase these leading products and services in the knowledge that owning them says an awful lot about them as people.

Service Leading Companies

The third and final type of company is the one that is primarily focused on the service it delivers to its customers. These companies may not necessarily have the leading products and they probably don't have the lowest prices but where they do excel is in the level of service and attention to detail they provide to their customers. In fact when you think about it they can't be a low-cost outfit and provide the best service because the level of profitability generated from a low-cost model will

---

1 There is no doubt that British Airways until recently has been a great example of a Product Leading Company. However, the success of the low cost airlines has forced them to change strategy and try to become both Product Leading and Price Leading. Typically companies that attempt to be all things to all men can often end up in a kind of business nomansland

often not generate enough revenues to invest in providing a higher standard of service. As in the two previous types of companies it's appropriate to give you a couple of examples of companies that fall into the Service Leading category.

Shoppers at John Lewis, and their supermarket franchise Waitrose, appreciate the level of service that is offered in their stores and this is especially true of the John Lewis account card holders who will often recommend to their friends the high level of customer services that they receive. The same is true of The Virgin Group and the travel company Kuoni who, whilst offering what are often very similar if not identical products to their customers, do offer difference in terms of the service that they provide to their customers. And as is the case with the Product Leading Companies, their customers are happy to pay a premium for that level of service.

So there are three types of company in terms of where their main focus is: Product, Price or Service. How about those companies that attempt to focus on two or even all three of the disciplines? Well, according to Fred Weirsema and William Treacy, the best-selling authors of *The Discipline of Market Leaders*, these companies are few and far between. A customer who demands the lowest possible price is most likely to shop around and except certain limitations in terms of product technology and service performance. Other customers whose preference is to own the best possible product will appreciate that a leading product will often come at a premium in terms of price. So, too, that of the customer who demands a level of service that's above what's normally acceptable.

The fact is these three types of company that we have described are at odds with each other and therefore it's difficult to find a company or supplier that offers a leading product available at the lowest price with a level of exceptional service both at the point of the sale and afterwards.

So what has this to do with the job of selling? There are two points we wish to make.

Firstly, by having a clear understanding of what type of company and/or product you are or have and whether you sell and market yourself primarily on the strength of your product, your service or your price, you can immediately make plans to ensure that the customers you sell to are the ones who are most likely to be attracted to your company type.

After all, if Harrods had a travel agency it would be more likely to sell a Kuoni holiday rather than an easyJet flight. Similarly high-profile product leading brands such as, let's say, expensive imported foodstuffs or designer fashion brands are most likely to be found in stores that present themselves in a similar high-profile leading fashion.

Now this doesn't mean that you focus solely on the group of customers that best fit the company and product offering you represent but it certainly means that's where you should go first. The full title of our book is *Sold! How to make it easy for people to buy from you*. Often the simplest way of achieving this is by making sure that the customers and prospective customers you interact with are those who appreciate and are in broad agreement with your offering, whether it is mainly based on being a leading product, a leading service or on the lowest possible cost.

Once you have exhausted this first group or choice of customers you can then look to use the ideas contained in this book to further increase your sales revenues with other customers. But the message here is straightforward. Start where you are strong. Start in places where it is not only going to be easy for your customers to buy from you but where it is also easy for you to sell to them.

The second point we wish to highlight is in terms of how and where you generate your business. It's generally accepted that there are only three methods of generating sales.

The first is simple. You sell to new customers, ones that have never experienced or tried your product before. There are a number of ways you can do this. Some methods involve extensive advertising, mailings or just knocking on new doors. One of the most effective ways though is through recommendation – that is, getting your existing customers to sell for you or ask them if they know anyone who would be interested in your products and services. This is one of the most cost-effective and time-efficient ways of generating new custom. You just have to remember to ask.

The second and third methods concern selling to your existing customers and involve either selling them more products or selling them same amount of products and asking them to purchase those products on a more frequent basis.

For example, a customer may purchase a specific product from you on a quarterly basis. One way of increasing sales would be to get the customer to buy this product every two months rather than every three. The alternative would be to ask them to purchase another product from your range. The same point can be illustrated by taking an example from the hotel and catering industry.

A customer may use your hotel or restaurant on an infrequent basis. Here your focus would be on turning them from an infrequent customer into a more frequent one. Using the straightforward and practical approach outlined in this book will help you do this effectively and will subsequently make it easier for your customer to buy more from you. The second way to increase your revenues in this instance would be to ask the customer to purchase something additional whilst you have their custom. This could take the form of a room-upgrade, a bottle of wine at dinner or any other additional product. Called 'adding on', selling to an existing customer is one of the most cost-effective and profitable ways to increase sales revenues.

We are reminded of a story about the merits of 'adding on' concerning a large chain of fast-food restaurants. The manager in this particular restaurant knew the obvious benefits of selling to his existing customer base. One of the ways he'd accomplish this was to ensure that all of the serving staff in his team would ask customers if they would like anything else while they were there. Anything else would comprise of extra french-fries, a drink such as a milkshake or perhaps a dessert. One day while showing a new member of serving staff the ropes he talked to his new employee, a young man, about the importance of asking customers while he was serving them, if there was anything else they would like to buy. The young gentlemen, keen to impress his new boss, took this idea to heart and made a conscientious effort to ask every customer he served whether they'd like to add a dessert to their order. After familiarizing himself with his work surroundings and aware that his manager was watching him from the side of the counter he began 'adding on'.

Customer after customer would approach the counter and after smiling at them, welcoming them to the restaurant and taking their order the young man would inquire politely whether they would like a dessert with their order. Customer after customer would decline and after half an hour he had succeeded in selling only one extra dessert. Feeling rather despondent he was clearly surprised when his manager approached him after half an hour and remarked on what a great job he was doing and how impressed he was with his efforts.

'But in half an hour I've only sold one dessert,' said the young man.

'That may be the case,' replied the restaurant manager, 'but at least you're asking everyone!'

The manager went on to explain that if every one of the serving staff, of which there were 20 or so, sold an extra dessert every half an hour – a restaurant that was open almost every day for 24 hours a day could sell an extra 350,000 desserts in a year. Just by simply asking! Herein lies an important message.

Every day there are thousands and thousands of sales people who are wasting a mountain of opportunities to sell more to their existing customers. Store assistants, garage attendants, field sales representatives, account managers, customer service agents – regardless of the sales role, the sales environment or the product – opportunities for additional sales are wasted. And there is often a simple remedy to make the most of these opportunities. That is simply asking the customer if they would like to buy.

For those who manage sales teams there is another important lesson that can be taken from this story. The restaurant manager, rather than get frustrated at his new recruit's inability to sell more than one dessert in half an hour, actually praised him for at least asking customers if they would like to buy one. We're sure that this young apprentice will continue to ask customers whether they'd like a dessert based on his manager's enthusiastic praise, the reason being that what gets positively reinforced tends to get repeated.

So your company is either Price Leading, Product Leading or Service Leading and you generate sales either by selling to new customers or getting your existing customers to buy both more and/or different products or by buying more frequently from you. Now an interesting thing happens when we look at these two elements together. For example, if you were representing a company whose primary focus was to deliver to your customers the lowest possible price (let's for the sake of argument call you No Frills

Limited) and you know that there are only three ways to generate extra sales revenue, which would you choose?

Can you sell your existing customers more products? Well, you probably could but bear in mind that they chose you because you deliver the lowest cost and it might be that they only have a finite budget, which is the primary reason they buy from you. In this instance while it's possible for them to buy more it might not be the easiest option for you or for your customer.

Could you get your existing customers to buy the same but more frequently from you? Well again it's possible but the same is true. Customers with a finite budget will tend not to have the additional resources to spend more often with you.

Customers with a finite budget will tend not to have the additional resources to spend more often with you.

So that leaves one option. Attracting and selling to new customers. In the case of No Frills Limited this is probably going to be their best option, and the ideal place to attract new customers is from their current base of customers, simply asking if they can refer you to others or recommend friends, family and colleagues, along with sales and marketing campaigns that appeal to the cost-conscientious customer. In this instance a sales person representing a Price Leading Company should, as part of their sales plan, include a request for a reference or referral, from every customer that they interact with.

Now what about the types of companies that we have described as being Product Leaders. Where are they most likely to generate their additional sales revenues? Are they most likely to find the easiest growth from new customers or will that revenue be more forthcoming by selling either more product or more frequently to their existing ones?

Again all three options are viable but in the case of the Product Leading Company possibly the easiest option would be to generate growth from their existing customer base. Often this customer base will be more discerning and have the resources to purchase new product offerings and ideas and therefore would be a good target audience in which to sell more product or encourage more frequent purchases. Sony understands these strategies well and spends a lot of time and effort in selling the latest ranges of video games or audiovisual equipment to a vast legion of Sony followers. Again whilst it is possible for Product Leading Companies to benefit from any of the three methods of generating sales discussed, concentrating on their current and already converted customers is in all likelihood going to be the most productive. This is reinforced by the fact that it is often up to five times more difficult (therefore read *more expensive!*) to attract a new customer than it is to maintain and sell more to an existing one. Which leaves us with the Service Leading Company.

Whilst any of the three methods are valid, the Service Leading Company is most likely to generate its easiest additional sales revenues from its existing customer base. These customers are already familiar with the overall level of service from the companies concerned and are therefore more likely to be responsive to new product lines, services and the like. One of the best examples of this in practice is the phenomenal success of UK supermarket retailer Tesco and its Clubcard Loyalty and Service Programme.

As a supermarket retailer Tesco quickly realized that by understanding and becoming intimate with its customers it could provide for them additional products and services that 'fitted' particular customer profiles. The Clubcard, a loyalty card that awards 'money off' vouchers and other incentives to shoppers, provides Tesco with an extensive volume of data and information about the personal habits and traits of each of its millions of Clubcard holders. By understanding this information Tesco is then able to segment its customers and offer personalized products and services that match or are in line with the personal profile of the customer. It has applied this level of customer service in order to drive sales in other traditionally non-food products and services including financial and insurance services.

The identification of whether a company is a Price, Product or Service Leader, and the impact this has on the types of customers it attracts and does business with, will certainly make it easier for the person in a sales role to identify where they are most likely to generate sales and growth.

So armed with product and industry knowledge, a belief about what you can achieve and what your products and services can deliver to a customer who has the need and the resources available, we're almost ready to examine the five Effective Selling Principles that make up *Sold!* Before we do, it's worth taking a closer look at a group of people that are often overlooked in the quest for finding new and profitable customers – and that's our existing ones. One of the most effective ways of selling is to sell to existing customers and yet this is where a number of companies and sales people can sometimes go wrong. Let's take an example that happened to us a few months ago when we were flying back to Heathrow after a weekend away. For the purposes of this story we will appoint a pseudonym for the airline we flew with ... let's call them ... KL ... erm ... N! After landing at Heathrow and proceeding through customs we went to the baggage hall to reclaim our bags. It quickly became apparent that a large number of customers on the flight were missing their bags. In fact there were about 20 people in total whose bags were missing from the flight. The voice on the tannoy instructed us to go to the airport lost baggage claim desk which we duly did. The sight of 20 customers approaching the desk was quite clearly too much for one of the airline representatives who scurried into the office at the back, leaving her colleague to deal with 20 frustrated and angry customers. And the airline's policy for dealing with this situation? We were all asked to fill out a form and give details of what our baggage looked like and where our final destination was and the like, only then would they deal with the situation. As you can imagine all this did was serve to create even more frustration in those people whose bags were lost. This was further fuelled by the way we were looked at by the airline representative when someone asked if they had any spare pens for filling out the form. After giving us her 'what do you think I am, a bloody stationer?' look, we managed to find three or four pens that we could share to fill out the forms.

At first glance you might just consider this to be poor customer service. We'd consider it to be poor selling. Here's why. The 20 people who had their baggage lost by this airline were already customers and, given the well-held view that selling to existing customers is easier and more cost-effective than attracting new ones, this airline did a pretty poor job of making sure that we remained customers and bought from them again. The irony is that this company had already done the hard work, it had already attracted our custom. All it needed to do was ensure that it kept it. Its very processes and systems ensured that it never would. Now, we may be looking at this a little too simplistically but, to our minds, it shouldn't take a genius to work out that the lost baggage claim desk at any airport for any airline is most likely to be visited by customers who are a little upset. Yet the whole system and process for dealing with these customers is to upset them even more by asking them to fill out forms without giving them any explanation as to what's going to happen. Surely the more sensible thing to do is to immediately admit up front that the company has done something wrong. 'Look guys, yes, we've lost your bags, here, sit down and have a cup of coffee while we explain all of the things that we are going to do to get your bags back to you as quickly as possible.' But oh no, the forms take over, the process takes over – and the end result? Twenty highly irate people who will need some serious convincing before using that airline again. The company focused on how to make its own life easier rather than its customers'. The irony is though that in the longer term the airline's life is going to be more difficult because the more they deal with customers in this way, the more infinitely difficult it will make it to attract these customers back to their products and services in the future.

Point made! Let's assume that you *do* have customers that you can sell to. What can you do to make it easier for them to buy from you?

Introduction

We all need sales people. From the dawn of time our very existence is based on our ability to trade, sell, influence and persuade. However, things are getting out of control.

With everyone's lives getting increasingly complex it's important that a vitally important role such as selling doesn't become complex too. But it has. There are hundreds of sales books describing thousands of tips and techniques to sell to customers but does all this clutter and complexity actually make it easier for our customers to buy from us? The people element seems to get forgotten.

The Effective Selling Principles take way all the non-essential ideas, tips and tactics that have complicated the approach to selling and provides you with just a few essential ideas across five principles that will make the difference for you and for your customer.

Those principles are:

1. Creating a well-formed sales goal, or what we also refer to as *'Getting ready'*

2. Creating and maintaining a valuable customer relationship, or *'Liking and listening'*

3. Establishing what is valuable to the customer, or *'Being productive'*

4. Providing what is valuable to the customer or, *'Giving 'em what they want'*

5. Gaining a commitment to action or *'Sold!'*

It's an approach that we believe will allow you to become more sophisticated by doing things more simply – and often doing less!

Whilst *Sold!* explains these essential principles, there are a few prerequisites that every person in sales should either have or be aware of in order to be successful. We should have belief in ourselves and in our products. We must have good levels of product knowledge and we should ensure that, as best we can, we're selling to the right customer, as some types of customers are more likely to buy from us than others.

There are also different types of company related to how they present themselves to their customers. Price Leading Companies are those that focus on delivering the lowest possible price whilst Product Leader Companies are intent on delivering the best product to the customer. Service Leading Companies are those that are renowned for their excellent total customer service.

It's up to five times harder and more expensive to attract a new customer than it is to sell to an existing one.

Creating a well-formed
sales goal

**Creating and maintaining
a valuable customer relationship**

Establishing what is valuable
to the customer

Providing what is valuable to
the customer

Gaining a commitment
to action

Creating and maintaining a valuable customer relationship

Liking and listening

n any sales situation it makes good sense to not only create a valuable relationship with your customer but also to maintain it as well – after all, as we have already alluded to in the introduction, it's not just about today's sale. You want to create situations where customers come back to you (or at the very least you want to create situations where you can go back to them) time and time again. It has been estimated that it's five times harder and five times more costly, to attract new customers than it is to service and sell well to those you already have.

Much has already been written about how to create and maintain valuable relationships with customers. Indeed there's almost irrefutable evidence that the customers with whom you have the best working relationships are the customers who are most likely to be your most profitable customers. They are also the customers who are most likely to help you generate new custom through referrals and endorsements. Many organisations realize this and spend vast amounts of time, resources and money in training and developing sales and customer staff to become more skilled and proficient at creating valuable relationships with customers yet the evidence points to the fact that they're still not very good at it. Now that's not to say you don't have customers who you do have great relationships with. Of course many of you have those types of customers. The type of customers who are always pleased to see you or speak to you. The type of customers that don't object about the cost of your product or the amount of time it will take to deliver. These are the sorts of people that are a pleasure to do business with. But they tend to be the minority. In fact Professor Malcolm Macdonald of Cranfield University found that in a survey he conducted of buyer and seller relationships, only 2 per cent of buyers rated the relationships they had with key suppliers as very good.[1] The great majority of buyers rated the relationships with their suppliers as, at best, quite good, with 62 per cent describing them as neither good or bad. This is startling. With the obvious benefits of creating and maintaining a valuable relationship with customers six out of ten of them describe their opinion of the relationship as indifferent.

---

1. 'Management Research in Practice – Building on Supplier and Buyer Perspectives Report', Financial Times/Prentice Hall.

What's also interesting to note is that a similar study looked at the amount of time it took to develop these valuable relationships. Perceived wisdom might lead us to think that the best relationships are time-dependent but that is simply not the case. There's no evidence to suggest that the longer the relationship is maintained the more likely a customer is to either continuing buying from you or to refer your products and services to new potential customers. We live in a fast-moving and ever-changing world. We have a greater number of relationships with a larger group of people often for shorter periods of time. The message here is about complacency – it is something that no sales person can afford to have. The message is simple – what are you going to do with your customers today that will ensure that they are your customers tomorrow?

What are you going to do with your customers today that will ensure that they are your customers tomorrow?

Clearly then the importance of creating and maintaining a valuable relationship with your customers has obvious advantages. But the irony is that our complex and cluttered world doesn't only create confusion and complexity for your customers. It also creates confusion and complexity for the sales person. There are literally hundreds, maybe thousands of tips, techniques and methods that could help you to create and maintain these relationships. So how *do* you create and maintain such valuable relationships? And do you really have to learn hundreds of different techniques for what, on the face of it, should be relatively simple and straightforward steps, or are there in fact just one or two things that you can focus on that will make the difference?

In order to answer all these questions there is a question that we should ask of ourselves, 'What makes a good customer?' And conversely, 'What makes a difficult customer?'

Here's a little exercise that will help. It should only take a few moments.

Think about one or two of your best customers and describe the things they do and the way they behave that makes them the best customers. If you have no one in particular then think about and describe a type of customer that you would consider being a good customer. You may like to write down a few of your thoughts before turning your attention to what, in your opinion, makes a difficult customer.

MY CUSTOMERS

MY 'GOOD' CUSTOMERS 😊	MY 'NOT-SO-GOOD' CUSTOMERS ☹

Everyone working in any sales or customer service environment probably has customers they get on well with – the sort of customer who is easy to do business with. They are understanding, they listen and they take on board your ideas. They never complain, they're always happy with the products and services you provide them with and they're more than prepared to tell their friends and colleagues about how good you are. They are a joy to work with and they make your job worthwhile.

Contrast this person with the difficult customer. You know the one. This is the customer who never listens to your point of view, never seems to listen to the advice you're trying to give them. They never seem to look you in the eye or treat you like a human being. To them you're just another item on their agenda that has to be dealt with. These are the sort of people who sometimes cause you to ask yourself: is it all worth the hassle?

As you look at the list of words and the descriptions you have used to describe what makes a good customer and what makes a difficult one, ask yourself the following questions:

- What do you notice about the relationship between yourself and the customers you rate as good ones?
- What do you notice about the relationship between yourself and the customers you rate as difficult?

These questions tend to stimulate a number of responses relating to the feelings you have about your customers and the relationships that you have with them. Generally you tend to evaluate how good or how difficult a customer is by the way they make you feel. Those customers you consider to be good customers tend to make you feel good about yourself. They listen to you and treat you in an understanding and respectful way. The difficult ones are often the complete opposite. The fact is that the customers you rate as good are the ones you tend to share the most similarities with and ones that you *like*. Similarly, these customers tend to like you in return and it's here that you find your first clue to how to quickly and effectively create and maintain valuable relationships with all your customers – we call it *liking*.

Liking

It'll probably come as no surprise that you tend to like people who, in turn, like you. In fact you also like more those people who tell you that they like you and a number of well known companies use the very notion of friendship and liking in order to generate their sales revenues. We are talking, of course, of the party plan environment, where a whole host of products ranging from cosmetics to . . . erm . . . adult stuff[1] are sold in homes across many countries of the world. And if you think about it for a few moments the setting is ideal for generating sales revenues. A group of like-minded people, talking, laughing and having a great time while the hostess of the party tops up glasses and hands round nibbles before turning their attention to the products on offer at that evening's event.[2]

What makes this setting so successful is the fact that most people don't feel that they are buying products from a faceless company. They actually feel they are buying from someone they like. The neighbour or the friend that invited them.

So what's the lesson here? Are we suggesting that we replace all our sales activities, retailing, advertising, sales forces and the like with the party plan concept? Clearly not. But we're suggesting that we look at what's creating the sales being made in the party plan environment – the fact that the people *like* each other. The valuable relationships are already created and even in situations where previous relationships don't exist and some people are meeting for the first time, the party organizers arrange for those relationships to be created through the simple process of chatting, exchanging information, and sometimes even playing games. The success lies in the creation and maintenance of a valuable relationship during the sale through the process of liking.

What causes liking?

So, surely the way to create and maintain valuable relationships with your customers is to find ways that you can get to like them and they in turn can

---

1. We didn't really know how to describe these products. We do not set out to offend anyone and sorry Ann Summers.
2. By the way we have *never* been invited to one of these parties. We'll be by the letter-box waiting for the invitations to flood in (hopefully).

like you? Well, yes, in fact it's often this simple. But before we get carried away let's just be clear about what we mean by 'liking' because one thing we're not advocating is that you and your customers all take a house together by the sea. What we are advocating though is that you do a little detective work to find out what would give you the best opportunity of liking your customers and in turn being liked. So, what things should you look out for? Fortunately the answer to this question can be found in the world of social science and in particular the work of a friend and colleague of ours, Professor Robert Cialdini PhD who is Professor of Psychology at Arizona State University and a fellow of the American Psychology Association.

Professor Cialdini has dedicated many years of his life into researching how one person can be persuaded to say yes to another and in his research he has identified six universal principles of persuasion, one of those principles being the principle of liking. He has not only proven that one person liking another is a powerful way of creating a persuasive and valuable relationship, he's also researched what causes one person to like another person. What this means for those of you working in the sales environment is that you have a very simple and easy-to-follow means by which you can begin to create and maintain valuable relationships.

So what causes one person to like another? There are three specific elements:

- Similarity
- Praise
- Co-operation

Let's take each in turn.

Similarity

All around us there are examples of how similarity causes us to like people more and often the similarities are quite simple ones: dressing in a similar fashion, supporting the same football or rugby team, living in the same part of town or having children of a similar age, for example. A classic similarity study conducted in the 1970s found that people were more likely to sign a petition supporting a particular political cause if they were asked to sign that petition by someone dressed in a similar fashion to themselves.

What was remarkable about this study was that those who signed were not actually told at any point what the petition was about.

Many companies are aware of the importance that similarity has on producing liking and in some cases will encourage their sales people to point out similarities they have with their potential customers. Some insurance and financial sales people, on discovering information about their customers' birth place or job might shortly afterwards reveal the fact that they, or a close member of their family, were also born in the same town or nearby. Car sales people might enquire about any sporting interests a prospective customer has or whether they have children only to amazingly, a short time later, mention that they too enjoy a round of golf but find it difficult these days with the pressures of bringing up a young family.

Now while there's absolutely no harm in mentioning genuine similarities that you share with your customers, it could be very harmful indeed to mislead a customer into believing that you share similarities that are actually not genuine. There are two major reasons for this.

Firstly, the Effective Selling Principle says that you should not only create but also maintain valuable relationships with your customers. Whilst fake similarities may serve to create a relationship, there will come a point in time when the customer will discover that you pulled the wool over their eyes for your own personal gain and this will only ensure that any relationship that was created will not now be maintained. The second reason is the fact that by creating a false impression of similarity you actually miss the opportunity to find out where you share genuine similarities. You literally miss the chance to share information, ask a few questions and seek out where true similarities exist. It is therefore important that you do your best to plan a little time at the beginning of your interactions with customers to engage in something that's often overlooked in our fast-moving world – *smalltalk*. It is here that a little preparation and planning is necessary. You may need to schedule those few extra minutes to ensure that you can find out enough about your customer or potential customer to create the valuable relationship you know to be so important. But what of those who just like to get down to business? Those who haven't the time (or give you the impression they don't have the time) to indulge in a little social foreplay? Well, for these people, the answer lies in a question normally found in the equine world: *'What's the best way to ride a horse?'* The answer is clearly that you ride a horse *in the direction the horse is going*. The same is true with those customers who just want to cut to the chase and get on with business. They want you to go in a certain direction (getting on with the sale) and by doing as the customer wishes (actually getting on with the sale) you do much to create a relationship by signalling that you have heard the customer and will show your similarity by cutting to the chase.

Praise

We all like praise. We love to hear people paying us compliments, it gives us that kind of warm feeling inside. The kind of feeling that says 'I like this person'. And it's true, as Professor Cialdini's research helpfully points out, we're more likely to like those who pay us compliments and give us praise. But surely we're not advocating that you all become the stereotypical cheesy, smiling, door-to-door salesman? Whatever next? you might be wondering. Kissing babies? Planting memorial trees in customers' gardens? No, of course not. But in the

same way that finding out about genuine similarities can help to create liking, so can genuinely praising customers. What can you compliment them on? Well, most things really, as long as you are sincere. It could be the fact that they are already a good customer – maybe you can compliment them on that fact. Perhaps, in the case of business-to-business sales, there are some things that your customer has achieved that you're especially impressed about. In the case of selling direct to consumers you may have some personal compliment that you could use to begin to create that valuable customer relationship. It can also be used to repair relationships that are maybe not going as well as you'd planned. Let's take an actual real-life example from a friend of ours who was having a little trouble at work with a colleague. It was one of those situations where this person would just rub our friend up the wrong way, possibly without even realizing they were doing it. Our friend was getting increasingly agitated about the relationship and, when it was first suggested that maybe they should focus on some of the things they liked about their colleague and possibly even tell them those things, our friend was not at all sure. However, as time went on, and the relationship became more and more stressed, our friend decided to give the compliment tactic a try. Their colleague, whilst irritating, did have a huge work ethic and was renowned for always delivering a first-class job on time all the time and it was here that our friend decided to focus her genuine praise. After telling her colleague that she admired the fact that he was able to work so effectively in delivering the work projects he was involved in, something changed about the way he interacted with our friend. Did they become friends? Certainly not. Are they friends now? No. But they did begin to create a relationship where they were able to work better together and get things done together. All through the use of a little homework and a genuine compliment.

Co-operation

The third element that causes people to like each other more and therefore helps to create valuable relationships is co-operation. We're sure that we won't surprise anyone by saying how important it is to show understanding and co-operation with customers. Why then do some companies and their sales people create environments where co-operation appears to be the last thing on their mind? We are talking here about the types of companies who almost treat the business of selling as a war. We have chosen the word 'war' carefully and it is highly appropriate. Take, for example, just a handful of things we have heard sales people (some very senior) say in the last few months:[1]

‘When the customer objects, it's our job to "argue" with them the case for our product.’

‘Attack the competition at every opportunity. Let our customers be under no illusion that we will "conquer" them and we "will" win the business that is rightly ours.’

‘Don't just sell for today – nail 'em down for ever!’

---

1. We kid you not!

'Customer objections are nearly always false ones. It is our job to over-come our customers.'

'Don't just sell – blow 'em away.'

Whilst a competitive environment is a healthy environment, it's important that over zealousness doesn't serve to destroy the very thing that will make you more competitive – the fact that you have valuable and co-operative relationships with customers. There has been much talk of the value and importance of 'stickiness' in customer relationships where your relation-ships with customers are sufficiently co-operative that they become 'sticky' – much like a personal relationship. The relationship becomes valuable and maintains its value because both the company and the cus-tomer realize that they achieve more by working together than by working in isolation. How much more business revenue can be achieved by work-ing in this way? We certainly believe that the potential is much greater by co-operation rather than approaching customers as some form of enemy, a barrier that needs to be overcome. Fine if you want to think of your com-petitors in this way, but again we have a word of warning. We have wit-nessed many occasions where companies and sales people who have focused on their competitors have invariably ended up behind them! Spending much of their time dealing with the competition and not actually dealing with the main players – the customers themselves. But that's another story. For the moment let's concentrate on how co-operating with customers will help create liking which will subsequently help you to create and maintain valuable relationships with customers that will give you the competitive advantage.

The evidence for co-operation in the business of selling is indeed strong and here we offer a compelling piece of research that supports our claim. A negotiation study conducted by Neil Rackham over a nine-year period sought to find an answer to the question, 'What do the most skilled nego-tiators do that makes them so much more successful than average negotiators?' In particular, the study looked at how the skilled negotiators prepared for their negotiations compared to those considered to be just average negotiators. One finding from the study clearly indicates the importance of finding ways of co-operating with customers and the sub-sequent success that follows. Whilst preparing for the negotiation the average negotiators spent most of their time, over 90 per cent of their time in fact, focusing and preparing for their own case, constructing their arguments and thinking about how they would defend their own position. Contrast that with the skilled negotiation group who spent 40 per cent of their time doing something of vital importance – looking for areas of shared interests. They were looking for common ground between themselves and the people with whom they were negotiating. In other words, they were looking for where they could agree and co-operate. Only when they'd sought that potential common ground did they then spend the remaining 60 per cent of their time preparing a negotiation plan that aligned with those areas of possible co-operation. A powerful message indeed and one that those of us in the business of selling should be well aware of.

You may have your own agenda in terms of the products and services that you need to sell. However, also think of what your customers' agenda may be. What is or could be important to them? What are they looking to achieve? And how might your product or service help them? This additional piece of thinking prior to a sales interaction can make the difference between pitching up and just 'tell selling' to your customers and actually making it easier for them to buy from you.

We know that creating and maintaining a relationship that both the customer and the sales person consider to be valuable is a vital part of the sales process. We know that this relationship not only allows the sales dialogue to progress, it can also create a competitive advantage for the selling company in terms of maintaining the relationship to the extent where the customer will return again and again. By looking for areas where you share similarities with the customer, are able to give them genuine praise and compliments and doing some detective work in seeking out areas where you can co-operate and collaborate with them you're well placed to create these valuable relationships. With *liking* mastered, it's time to take a look at the other element that creates and maintains valuable customer relationships – *listening*.

Listening

A few years ago a friend of ours was looking to buy a new car and asked one of us to go along and help her. Our friend was terribly excited at the prospect of buying a new car and, as a customer, she had done her homework. She already had a good idea of how much her current car was worth and she had worked out that this trade-in value, together with money she had in a savings account and a bank loan she had been offered she could probably afford to buy a brand new car. Or at least a very good nearly-new car. She also had a really good idea of what she was looking for because when we asked her she said that she wanted a car that was a bright and vibrant colour and that looked different to the car she currently owned.[1] She went on to tell us that it needed to have power steering which her current car didn't have, a cool sounding stereo and . . . at this point she made a pressing action with her right hand and said 'chunk, chink'.[2]

We thought about the different car dealers that were located in the area and couldn't help thinking that one of them was going to have a very easy time selling this lady a motor car. She had the need for a new car, had a very clear idea of what she was looking for and had the cash to pay for it. A sales person's dream. Oh, how wrong we were!

The day started disastrously. Our first port of call was a car dealer where she never actually got to speak to anyone. The person at the sales desk was on the telephone at the time, simultaneously chewing the top of his pen and with his feet up on the desk. He looked over in our direction and gave us a kind of 'I'll be with you in a minute' sign whilst at the same time telling us  to have a look around the showroom. Well, at least we took that to be what he meant – this gentleman clearly didn't play charades at Christmas.

So, after having a look around for 15 minutes or so and occasionally giving the salesman an impatient looking glance, which was reciprocated each time with the 'honest, I'll only be another minute or two' sign, we left. On to car dealer number two where we did get to speak to someone. The

---

1. At the time she owned a small hatchback – we knew what she meant, as a lot of them *do* look the same!
2. 'Chunk, chink' was her way of indicating remote central locking. This is important as we will see later.

problem was that while our friend was interested in speaking to the sales person, the sales person didn't appear too interested in talking to our friend. What he was interested in doing was talking to us. Our friend muttered under her breath what we thought at the time was a well-justified comment about 'bloody men!' before declaring that she would take her custom elsewhere. And so it went on. And on. Car dealer after car dealer who didn't seem to get the fact that here was a customer who knew what they wanted and just needed someone to listen to her.

'No, I don't want to talk about the finance deals', she said at the third time of being asked (amazingly by the same sales person). 'I have the cash.'

'Actually I'm not really interested in this one as I did say I needed "Chunk Chink" remote locking!'

Close to tears, partly of frustration and partly due to the fact that her dream of buying a car, which she thought might be a pleasurable experience, was not happening for her, she decided to go home. It was on the way back that we passed another car dealer that we had yet to visit. She needed to be persuaded to stop and see if they were any different from the other showrooms we had visited that day. Fortunately they were.

'Hello. How can I help you?'

'I'm looking for a new car and I know what I want and how much money I have to spend.'

'OK. What do I need to do?'

'Show me a car that doesn't look like a Vauxhall Corsa, is a bright colour, has a cool stereo, remote locking and doesn't cost more than £12,000.'

'Come with me', came the reply, as the sales person took her towards a car at the rear of the showroom. 'This doesn't look like a Vauxhall Corsa, it's bright red and has a great sounding stereo and ...' he pointed a key fob towards the car, pressed the button and it was there for her to hear: 'Chunk Chink'.

Our friend smiled broadly. She had just bought a new car.

We, though, are on to our next story.

Have you ever had the experience of someone reading back to you your phone number in a way that's different to how you remember it? It doesn't sound like your number, does it? It's almost as if the person who is reading it out hasn't listened to what you've said. It's like they've changed your phone number – and without your permission.[1] How does it make you feel? Frustrated? Annoyed? Why can't they just listen to what you said? And what does the fact that they appear not to have listened to you do to the relationship they have with you? Does it help to create and maintain a valuable relationship?

Of course not, and yet the ability to demonstrate that you have accurately heard what a customer has said to you and to be able to demonstrate that understanding is one of the most common mistakes made in sales.

Listening is not only one of the keys to success in sales but also life in general. Truly effective listening is the ability to give people your full attention and then demonstrating that you understand what that person is saying to you. As you are primarily concerned with the role listening plays in your ability to make it easier for your customers to buy from you it's essential that

Listening is not only one of the keys to success in sales but also life in general.

you understand its importance. Numerous surveys have found that customers rate being listened to and understood by a sales person as one of the most important criteria for determining whether they do business with a company or not. In fact a recent survey conducted by a consumer society suggests that, along with honesty and a sales person's product knowledge, the ability to listen to a customer's needs ranks in the top three things that are important to customers when they make a purchase. And this is not surprising. After all, think about it from the perspective of when you are the customer. Who would you rather do business with, the person who demonstrates that they genuinely want to understand and get to know more about you, your goals and your business or the person who is there simply to sell to you regardless of what you actually think?

---

1. For example, they read back to you 087–078–74747 instead of your 0870–787–4747

We have all been given two tools in which to receive verbal communication and only one to give out verbal communication so that may give us a clue as to the order in which we use them.

So how about a few ideas on being able to listen effectively and demonstrate understanding with our customers.

Firstly, you need to be ready to listen. If you try to listen and memorize what your customer is saying then your attention is not on them but on your own internal dialogue. It's almost like you are trying to listen to two people at the same time and the result could be that you lose not just potentially useful information but just as importantly an opportunity to show that you're being attentive and respectful.

Therefore it's important that you face your customer by standing or sitting symmetrically opposite to them. You should maintain good, but not persistent, eye contact and adopt a friendly, open posture and concentrate on the customer, not what you want your next killer question to be. As Stephen Covey, the author of *Seven Habits of Highly Effective People* says, 'seek first to understand and then to be understood'.

Secondly, you need to be fully aware of what you are hearing and the way you use the words you hear. For a few moments go back to the story of our friend and her experience of buying a new car. Time and time again she went to car showrooms with a clear idea of what she wanted. Not only was she clear about what she wanted, she was also happy to share her needs with any sales person who asked her. She was not a difficult customer although she quickly became a frustrated one because the people she was trying to deal with either didn't listen to her or chose to ignore or change what she said. And herein lies the most important element of listening. Use the same words that your customer uses in order to send a signal back to them that they have been heard. The car dealer who our friend eventually bought her car from did one thing that none of the other sales people that she dealt with did. He demonstrated he heard her by repeating back to her the exact same words that she used. He sent her the signal 'I have listened to you'. He literally played back to her the fact that she wanted a brightly coloured car, a cool sounding stereo that didn't look like the current car she owned. No changes, no deviation, just plain and simple playing it straight back. Her response? Sold!

Now, there is a school of thought that suggests that the best way to demonstrate that you have listened to someone is to 'paraphrase' back to them what they have said to you. We find this idea to be, well, frankly, barmy.[1] Our claim deserves an explanation.

Think about this sentence for a few moments:

The cat sat on the mat.

Think about what it means and visualize it.

What colour is the cat? Brown? Black? A tabby perhaps? What about the mat? Is it one of those big round Persian types or is it a plain old common or garden mat? The fact is that for everyone it will be slightly different. What is the same, though, are the words 'the cat sat on the mat' and here is reason why paraphrasing is not useful when attempting to demonstrate to someone that you are listening to them. We all attach incredible importance to the words that we use and we all attach specific and individual meanings to them. So when you're listening and demonstrating to someone that you've heard and understood them it's important that you use the same words, otherwise you are distorting what they have just said. If the customer says they want something that is cost-effective then they want something that is cost-effective. They don't want cheap or reasonably priced – they want cost-effective. They know what they mean and you have to demonstrate first and foremost that you have heard what they have said. You will certainly have to ask a follow-up question to get an understanding of what cost-effective means to them but the fact remains they are using the phrase 'cost-effective' and you should too. We therefore commend to you, the reader, a sales neologism,[2] that neologism being 'Parrotphrasing'. Parrotphrasing is concerned with using the same words as your customer and it is intuitive as something rather interesting happens when you parrotphrase: a customer says 'yes' to you more.

---

1. An old English slang word meaning 'crazy, silly and deranged'. Apparently the word originally came from something to do with yeast. We digress!
2. Meaning: made-up new word.

Remember the scenario when a person reads back your phone number differently to how you remember it yourself? You immediately think, 'that doesn't sound like my phone number'. Contrast that with someone who repeats it back exactly the way you said it. Your response is, 'Yes. That's right'. The same is true of our car-buying friend. The last sales person just repeated back what she had asked for and her response was, 'Yes'.

And here is probably the most important advantage of 'parrotphrasing'. It generates *yes* responses from your customers. What a great position to be in as a sales person – situations where your customers say yes to you.

We have a final note about listening and with it a neat way of making yourself much more effective at the skill. As well as two eyes, two ears and our mouths we also require two other tools. A pen and a piece of paper. There is something very productive about taking notes.

Taking notes can help you focus your attention on your customer. You won't be thinking up your next killer question or response while you're writing. Keeping notes means there is less chance of you missing something vital or important.

When you take notes you're demonstrating to your customer that you are paying attention to them. You're demonstrating that their opinions are important and this will create and maintain that all-important relationship. Taking notes means that you don't have to look them in the eye the whole time, which can become uncomfortable for some people.

For those of you who make repeated sales calls on your customers, having an accurate set of notes makes it easier to carry on your conversation the next time you speak to them. This will ensure that the relationship and your sales call will move forward each time rather than just remaining static. And your notes become a permanent record of the sales process. They literally become a contract for the next call and believe it or not can actually help to create commitments to action. Customers very often become less likely to change their mind when you produce notes from a last meeting or sales call.

Give note-taking a try. It will focus your attention on the customer and help you to develop a greater level of understanding with them.

Chapter 1 Creating and maintaining a valuable customer relationship
(Liking and listening)

Of the thousands of tips and techniques you can use to create and maintain valuable customer relationships, two are of the greatest importance – liking and listening.

Liking

People who like each other are more likely to get on (i.e. engage in and maintain a relationship) than those who don't. There are three specific things that cause liking:

- similarities
- praise
- co-operation.

Take some time to find out where you and your customers genuinely share things in common or are *alike*. This investment can pay you back many times over. Remember, you are dealing with human beings.

Listening

The best way to demonstrate you are listening to your customers is to use the same words and phrases that they do:

'parrotphrase' rather than 'paraphrase'.

If someone believes that you understand what they mean they will invariably say *yes* to you. Having your customers say *yes* to you is far preferable to them saying *no*.

Keep accurate notes and remember it's often more powerful to listen and understand than it is to persuade.

Creating a well-formed
sales goal

Creating and maintaining
a valuable customer relationship

**Establishing what is valuable
to the customer**

Providing what is valuable to
the customer

Gaining a commitment
to action

Establishing what is valuable to the customer

(Being productive)

ike many other people we enjoy the odd drink. You know the sort of thing, a couple of flasks of a popular Belgian brew on a Friday evening after a particularly stressful week in the office. Sometimes we enjoy more than the odd drink, generally reserved for the sort of occasions when we have something special to celebrate (you won't believe what justification we come up with for what is special). It was one such celebration that saw us sitting in a local public house recently. The pub itself was one of the more traditional pubs that we sometimes frequent as it's close to our office. The kind that serves good old honest beer and has little in the way of noisy distractions such as jukeboxes and pin-tables. We like this pub because it gives us the chance to relax and have a chat and we have even been known to come up with the odd idea for a training workshop while discussing life, the universe and everything, but on this particular evening we were somewhat distracted.

Pubs are great places to people-watch but on this evening it wasn't the people using the bar that we were focusing on, it was what was happening behind the bar that caught our eyes and ears. There was some employee training occurring and we couldn't resist the urge to eavesdrop.

The manager was showing the ropes to a new member of bar staff. This included him pointing out where everything was located, beer pumps, wines, spirits, soft drinks, the cash register and the like. The manager was especially keen to draw his new employee's attention to a laminated poster that was located on one of the walls behind the bar. He was not only successful at drawing the new employee's attention to this poster but also our attention, (although we did have to lean rather dangerously forward on our stools and stretch our necks out to see what this man was referring to). The poster in question, to which the bar manager pointed on at least three occasions to this new employee, contained a list of 'customer prompts' that included such things as, 'Always acknowledge the customer when they approach the bar', and, 'Smile in a friendly manner and ask the customer what they would like to order'.

All good stuff, we thought, even if the manager was a little obsessive in his pains to point out how important it was to follow the 'good customer service code'. So obsessive in fact that he at one point asked the new member of staff to recite the service code back to him as a test that they had well and truly got the message. Hmmm. We looked at each other and could almost predict what was going to happen next. We didn't have to wait that long. In fact it was just a few moments later when the manager proudly announced that the new member of bar staff was ready to serve some customers and the manager retreated to the end of the bar in order to witness his protégé's work.

Enter a young man who came up to the bar waving a note in his hand. 'Hello', said the bar attendant accompanying his greeting with the required smile:

'How can I help you?'

'Give us some change for the cigarette machine mate.'

'Would you like ice and lemon with that?' [1]

How foolish the person behind the bar appears for this quite inappropriate response. But are they actually the foolish one in this situation? Whatever way we look at what happened, they did what they were asked and what they did was the 'right' thing to do given the company's instructions that were so vehemently referred to by both the manager of the bar and the laminated poster itself.

They were right but were they effective or productive? An interesting question really, the question that asks if we would rather be right or effective. We have lost count of the number of times a sales person or a department in a company has done the 'right' thing and simultaneously dealt with the customer ineffectively and as a consequence either damaged the sale or lost tomorrow's. The airline example we referred to in the introduction is a good example of this. What was done was, according the rules, the right thing to do. But did it serve to create an effective outcome for the customers? Did the right thing to do produce future sales growth? We're not so sure.

So what has the story of the bar person got to do with the second of the Effective Selling Principles – the one we call establishing what is valuable to the customer? And what was it that caused this person to respond in

---

1. Yes this did actually happen. Even we couldn't make this up.

such an inappropriate way? Well there could be two explanations. The first one is that the person in question recognized how ludicrous it was to stick, word for word, to a script that, whilst useful in terms of a prompt, clearly wasn't a useful question to ask every customer that walked through the door and perhaps, upon recognizing this situation, they deliberately used the prompt sheet to point out how ridiculous it was in this particular circumstance.

The second explanation is that the bar manager had done such a good job drawing his employee's attention to the 'good customer service code' that he literally directed their attention to it at the expense of everything else. The message for the new employee was simple. Concentrate on the poster and remember it to the expense of everything else and to the expense of common sense.

You can direct a customer's attention by the way you ask them a particular question.

Regardless of which of these two explanations is the more likely they both contain a (fairly extreme) lesson for you which relates to how you, when you are selling, establish what is valuable to your customers. Only by establishing what that value is will you be able to see whether you can in fact provide that value which in turn will make it easier for the customer to buy from you.

The lesson is one relating to a very important skill in the business of selling – asking questions – and is simply this. You can direct a customer's attention by the way you ask them a particular question and where you place that customer's attention may be productive or unproductive to you and your customer's cause. Take an example by way of illustration.

If we were to ask you what you like most about the current car you drive, you would have to think about your current car and the things you like about it (assuming there are some things you like about it) in order to respond to the question. Similarly, if we were to ask you what might stop you from buying a car that we are trying to sell you, your attention would be directed to the things that stop you from buying the car.

'Which direction are your questions taking your customer?'

By asking someone a question you are literally directing that person's attention in a particular direction and therefore influencing the progress (or not) of the subsequent discussion that continues. This is important for two reasons. Firstly, because as sales people you ensure that the questions you ask are related to the needs of the customer and of yourselves and, secondly, because you need to deal appropriately with the response the customer gives you in order to move both the discussion and the sale forward in a productive manner.

In essence the questions that you ask your customers should fulfil only two criteria. They should be productive and they should ideally enhance the relationship or at the very least maintain the relationship you have created through liking and listening.

Being productive

So what do we mean by a productive question? Is it that one killer question that opens up the customer to the point where they spill out every want, need and desire on the table so you get the full story of what they, want thereby enabling you to present the features and benefits of your product? Or is it the sort of question that limits the information you glean from the customer to a few essential needs that your product can satisfy? After all it's entirely possible to ask questions in such a way that you get the answers you're looking for. A kind of solution looking for a problem if you like.

No. The answer is that productive questions are not necessarily the right questions at all. Productive questions are those that get you and your customer to a point that enhances the sales process. Productive questions move the sales person towards the point where they can sell their product or service to the customer and at the same time move the customer towards a point where it's easier for them to buy that product or service.

Remember: Would you rather be right or would you rather be productive?

So what of the classic 'open' and 'closed' question model so universally recognized by sales people? The one that defines closed questions as those that a customer can respond to with a simple one-word answer such as 'yes' or 'no'. Questions like:

'Is the cost going to be an important factor in making your decision?'

Answer: 'Yes.'

Whereas open questions are those where a customer has to answer with more than the tacit one worder such as:

'What are the important factors when considering making your decision?'

Answer: 'Well cost is important but so is reliability and a quick delivery time.'

Describing questions as open and closed whilst offering a useful definition as to two specific types of question may not, in hindsight, be that helpful because both can be as productive in certain sales situations as they are unproductive in others. Better, surely, to concentrate on asking the most productive question at the most productive time. Again, would you rather be right or would you rather be productive?

So let's return to the two questions we posed earlier as examples and see what is really happening when you ask them. For the first example, let's assume for a moment that you are a sales representatives for a car dealer talking with a potential customer who has walked into your showroom looking to purchase a new car.

You will remember that the first question went like this:

'What things do you like most about the current car you drive?'

Whilst you may be forgiven for thinking that this question makes the assumption that your potential customer does indeed like some things about their current car should they respond with the answer, 'Nothing!' at least you have a clue as to what question you should ask next. However, should your potential customer indeed like a few things about their current car, telling you what those things are will offer you some useful clues as to what they might be looking for in their new one. You simply need to repeat back those key likes parrotphrase style and enquire if they want similar features in their new car.

So is the question a productive one? When looked at in this way then the answer is invariably yes. It is productive because it elicits information that's useful to you as a sales person as a way of understanding what's valuable to the customer and it's valuable to the customer by way of confirming their needs. It is also productive in terms of maintaining a relationship with the customer because you've demonstrated that you have heard what is valuable to them. You have good information to plot the course of the sale with the customer and you've signalled to the customer what you have heard as being valuable to them. Productive indeed.

So what of our second example – the 'what stops you?' question. For the purposes of demonstration this time imagine yourself to be a representative of a computer hardware supplier who's demonstrating your company's latest bit of kit to an IT department manager in a medium-sized company. During the demonstration, which you are conducting with much excitement and enthusiasm you ask:

'So what things might cause you to stop purchasing a product such as this?'

As we have already pointed out any question you ask of a person will direct their attention in a certain way. Here the question is directing the IT manager's attention to things (possibly a long list of things) that will stop him from purchasing your product. Productive? Possibly, but also possibly not. Whilst the question will give you information about potential concerns or situations that prohibit the sale it does not necessarily follow that by dealing with these concerns or situations the sale of, in this case, computer hardware will automatically follow. The question is focused on what stops the sale progressing and therefore you have directed your potential customer's attention to the factors that will actually cause the sales process to falter or even cease all together. Productive? All of a sudden when viewed in this way, probably not.

It's not only unproductive in terms of where the question places your customer's attention, it also has the possibility of damaging any relationship you've created in the listening and liking stage. The reason for this stems from something that we'll refer to more in our chapter on gaining commitment but is worthy of mention here, albeit briefly.

When someone expresses an opinion or a belief about something, they invariably become more committed to that opinion or belief. This is especially true if the opinion or belief is expressed in front of others. In our example question, your potential customer has told you the things that will stop him from considering buying your product. These things could be related to the fact that he thinks your product is expensive or perhaps will involve an awful lot of training for his IT team which will take them away from important tasks that need to be delivered to quite tight deadlines. As a professional sales person, not only do you have a huge amount of knowledge about your product, you also have (or hopefully should have) belief and confidence in your product. Given this knowledge of and belief in your products you will probably be able to 'argue' the case for the merits of your product to the IT manager, and herein lies the danger. You might feel entitled to go to great pains to point out to the IT manager that your product actually doesn't require an awful lot of training and also that your product is certainly very cost-effective compared to some of the other options available.

The situation becomes one where you as a sales person are in one position and have a belief about one thing and your customer or potential customer is in another position with a different belief. This in itself is not disastrous; in fact it's commonplace. After all the very business of selling means you are often faced with situations where you need to convince others who have a belief or opinion that is different to yours. That's not the point we are making. What we do want to get across is how these situations arise in the first place and then how you deal with them.

In the example with the IT manager, the response you got was a direct result of the question you asked. You asked, 'So what things might cause you to stop purchasing a product such as this?' and the answer you got was a list of things that might stop him purchasing your product. Your question served only to focus your potential customer's attention on all the things that would stop him buying your product. Will a question like this make it easier for your customer to buy from you? Probably not, and it certainly creates additional problems for you because you then need to persuade your potential customer that the issues he thinks are valid reasons not to buy your product are not really too much of an issue after all.

Secondly, the way you present your 'counterarguments' to these potential issues could do much to potentially damage any relationship you have worked hard to develop in the earlier stages of the sales call. As we mentioned earlier, once we have a belief about something we tend to take a 'position' that could make it more difficult for others to persuade us differently. Indeed we have seen examples of where sales people have become defensive and on a few occasions have actually had arguments with customers because, get this, the customer answered the sales person's question with an opinion that was different to the sales person's belief. On a number of these occasions the sales person's opinion was actually the right one and the customer had got it wrong – but in hindsight, would the sales person rather have been productive in the first instance rather than just right?

Better, surely, that you avoid the situation altogether by thinking about what specific questions you need to ask before you see the customer and as a result have a clear idea of the types of responses your customers could give you to those questions. This is what we would call productive questioning skills and it is those productive questioning skills that will serve you well when establishing what is important to the customer.

What makes a productive question?

A productive question has two elements. Firstly, it's a question that gets you and your customers closer to an agreed outcome that's going to be valuable to both of you. And secondly it's a question that at the very least maintains the relationship you have created and at best enhances and improves upon that relationship. Thinking ahead about questioning in this way requires a little forward planning but it is time well invested as it can actually save both you and your customers time during the sales process and can help get you straight to the heart of what could be valuable to the customer. In turn this gives you the opportunity to make a reasoned decision about whether you can help them or not.

Thinking ahead about questioning requires a little forward planning but it is time well invested.

The graphic below illustrates what quadrant the questions you ask your customer should fall into. Too many questions in the wrong quadrant will ultimately mean that you are not being productive in the sale.

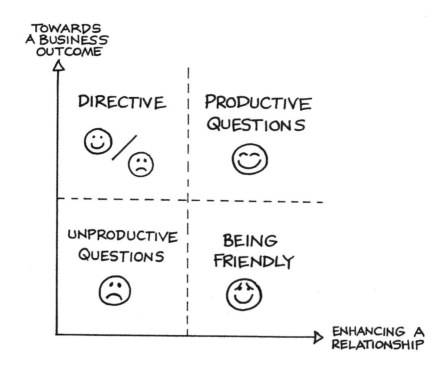

For example let's take the bottom-left quadrant which captures questions that enhance or develop the relationship you have with the customer but that are not necessarily productive in terms of generating business, questions like:

'Hi, how's it going?'

'How's the old golf handicap going? Have you played much lately?'

'How's the family and the kids? Has Johnny got to play in the School Football Team yet?'

'Did you buy that new car you were talking about last time?'

These kinds of questions serve a useful purpose, especially early on in a sales interaction because they give you the opportunity to create a relationship and dialogue with the customer. Creating that dialogue and relationship is important as the customer will be more likely to be responsive to the questions you ask when you get to the 'establish what is valuable to the customer stage'. So, all in all, questions that fall into the top left-hand quadrant are productive, but they do come with a warning.

Your business is selling and that makes customers your business because they are the ones who provide the sales revenues which in turn influence the success of the company you represent. But sometimes customers become more than just customers. You start to share more than just a business relationship with them and they become friends. They become the sort of people that you can call on in their office or business and see quite easily often even without an appointment . This situation in itself is fine; however, the warning bells start to ring when the relationship clouds the real purpose of why the relationship is there in the first place, that purpose being to get business done.

To some people the idea of selling to people they like and get on well with is one of the greatest rewards in sales. We are sure that, like us, you have some fabulous customers that you love working with and the fact that you get on well actually means you are successful doing business with them and they, in turn, are successful too. It is a really neat and efficient system.

But there are situations where some sales people do let the relationship get in the way of getting business done. In situations like this the sales person actually finds it difficult to sell to the customer because they fear that the relationship they have could get damaged if they start the 'shady' business of selling. An even worse scenario is when the customer actually uses the relationship with the sales person to avoid being sold to. We know of sales people who have asked us how to deal with customers who 'pretend' to be friendly with them in the hope that the sales person won't start selling to them. On further questioning we nearly always find out that even though there is very little chance of ever securing any business from these types of customers the sales people still religiously call on them every few months. Often the purpose of these sales calls is to achieve nothing more than the delivery of their company's latest leather-bound diary or perhaps a desk-tidy emblazoned with their corporate logo. They could save themselves the time and money by posting the gift or better still ask the customer outright if they are going to give them any business and following the response make a business decision about whether they should see that customer ever again.

On to the bottom-left quadrant that incorporates questions that neither move the sales process forward in a productive manner nor maintain or enhance the value of the relationship with the customer. It is apparent that questions that fall into this quadrant are clearly unproductive as far as following an effective sales process is concerned. However, rather than moving on rapidly it's appropriate to think about them for a few moments as it's the very idea of not thinking about them that causes them to be used. You're all busy people and you all have demands that sometimes cause you to just get on and do things without much thinking. Whilst there is often a real time-saving component to just getting on and doing the job, there is the danger that time saved today could cost you dearly in the future. Simply selling to a customer without any due consideration of what you're going to ask them, or worse still, asking a question that occupies the customer's mind long enough for you to think up another will result in inappropriate questioning that will be of no value to you or to your customer and will almost certainly mean that that customer will not be one for much longer.

But what about the questions that fall into our third quadrant – the one where you are asking business-focused questions but doing little to create or maintain a valuable relationship with the customer – are these productive or unproductive? The answer here, sorry to say, is that it all depends.

Some customers like the idea of just getting on with the business of doing business. You have probably met these kinds of customers on occasions in the past. They are sometimes described as direct, impatient, strong-willed or in extreme cases even aggressive. Dealing with this sort of customer requires careful handling but if you take your cue from the liking and listening elements in Chapter 1 you quickly realize that by being similar to them in the way they like to do business and being as directive as they are in the questions you ask can be very productive indeed. Where business-focused questions that do little to maintain, or in some cases actually damage, the relationship can be unproductive is in situations where you, the sales person, are seen to be direct, impatient or too aggressive in the way you approach and deal with the customer. On occasions like this your approach would clearly be unproductive and affords you a clear lesson when using questions that fall into this quadrant. If the customer is one of those direct and to the point types with little interest in building relation-ships and much interest in getting down to business then use the same approach. If on the other hand, though, it's you who prefers this approach, then you need to be aware of that fact and adapt accordingly to what's most valuable to the customer you're currently selling to.

Which takes us finally to the last quadrant that deals with questions that are business-focused and also at least maintain or better still enhance the relationship you have with the customer. These are the most productive of all. They focus both your own attention and also your customers on the business in hand in a way that makes the sales experience useful and even perhaps an enjoyable one.

We have discussed the idea that the questions you ask during a sales interaction with a customer can be productive or unproductive. We've also talked about the fact that some of the questions you ask are more likely to maintain or enhance the relationship you have with the customer. With that in mind let's take some specific examples of commonly used sales questions and judge how productive they really are.

Questions that ask about a customer's circumstances

Questions that ask about a customer's specific circumstances and situation can be either productive or unproductive depending on how you use them. You should always consider whether or not you really need the information you are asking for. We all know how annoying it is when you have to call a customer service centre or a helpline and then have to explain the reason for your call sometimes to three or four different people before you actually get to speak to someone who is in a position to be able to help you. It sometimes makes you wonder what entitles them to call themselves 'helplines'. The same is true when you are dealing with customers on a face-to-face basis. If you want to sell the customer a product or service, do you really need to ask lots and lots of questions to get information about their circumstances? Surely better that you do your homework in advance and ask only those questions that are pertinent to the sale and the customer you are interacting with. There is another point to make about questions of this sort and it relates to keeping accurate and up-to-date customer records. Having good up-to-date information to hand about your customers prevents you asking the same questions every time you sell to them. You can quickly check with just one or two questions that their circumstances are indeed the same and move on to more productive questions that move the sale forward. The obvious exception to this is if it's the first time that you've met the customer. In these situations some circumstantial information may be useful, but you need to be careful that it doesn't lead to a list of questions being fired at the customer in quick succession as this will probably have a detrimental effect on the relationship, with the customer feeling badgered.

Some examples of circumstantial questions:

- What products are you currently using to provide [insert whatever your product provides]?
- How many of these would you typically use in a [period of time].

Questions that get 'because' as an answer

Typically these questions start with the word 'why':

- Why have you bought a product like that in the past?
- Why do you use [insert name of competitor product]?

But there are other questions that take the customer in a similar direction:

- What caused you to choose a product like that in the past?
- What are your reasons for using [insert name of competitor product]?

Whether you use a question that starts with the word 'why' or another question that seeks to get the same information you need to be aware of a very specific effect that it can have on the customer, and therefore we should take great care when asking questions like these. The reason for this lies in the response that a customer is likely to give immediately after you ask the question, that response being the word 'because'.

So what are the dangers of asking questions that cause your customer to respond with the word 'because'. One danger is that your question might cause the customer to justify their position or point of view with regard to a decision they've already made and could already be committed to. And what if that position or point of view is different to the direction you would like the customer to move towards? By way of an example let's imagine you are in the following situation. You are selling to a customer who doesn't yet use your product, or perhaps they use just a small amount but certainly nowhere near the amount they could potentially buy from you. During your sales call you innocently ask the customer, 'Why do you use our competitor's product?' to which the customer replies, 'Because it's less expensive than your product, it's a good effective product that I have been using for over five years now and they have never let me down'.

> **One danger is that your question might cause the customer to justify their position or point of view with regard to a decision they've already made.**

The only thing you have successfully served to achieve by asking this question is to draw your customer's attention to the reasons why he uses your competitor's product. Productive? Probably not, as your sale will now more likely be focused on how you can sell against the product he already uses with you taking one side and your customer potentially taking the other. Herein lies the other potential danger. Your question will take the customer in the direction of having to justify a decision they have made. Whilst some customers might not have a problem with this, your relationship with the customer might only be in the early stages and you might be meeting this customer for only the first or second time. In these circumstances your question might only serve to ensure that you're unlikely to get his business anytime soon in the future.

We have painted a rather bleak picture of questions that get the customer to justify a particular position and whilst they are generally unproductive there are occasions when they can be very productive indeed. We are referring to situations when you have a customer that already uses and likes your products and services. In these situations asking them, 'Why do you like our product?' can serve to reinforce in the customer's mind why they like your product. This can be particularly useful when your sales objective is to increase their use of a product or if you're introducing a new product you have recently launched. Here the overriding message of this chapter appears once more. Only by preparing in advance and thinking about what you want to achieve and the types of questions you will use are you more likely to get you and your customers into a position where a successful sale can occur.

Questions that stop the sales process (inactive questioning)

We talked about this type of question earlier but it's worth reviewing because, as well as providing us with a lesson about what not to do, you can also get some very helpful clues about what you should be doing instead. For this reason let's go back to the IT manager we were talking about earlier. Remember you asked him, 'So what things might cause you to stop purchasing a product such as this?'

As a result of this question your potential customer gave you a list of things that would stop him from buying from you. Not only is this question unproductive because it actually stops the sales process, it's unproductive in another way too. Even if you're able to deal effectively with the IT manager's reasons why he won't buy your product it doesn't necessarily mean that he will now proceed with buying your product.

To illustrate this point, imagine, for a few minutes, that you're in your car approaching the top of a road that has a large junction with a set of traffic lights. What are the things that cause you to stop your car? Well, clearly, if the traffic lights are showing red you would stop (assuming that you are not driving in central London). The fact that you place your foot on the break will cause your car to stop, as will the car in front of you which has also stopped (assuming this time that you wish to avoid an accident which, by the way, will also cause you to stop).

So, in this situation there are three things that will cause you to stop your car:

- a red light showing on the traffic lights
- your foot on the break
- the car in front.

Now let's just imagine for a few moments that you're at the junction and a helpful young man comes and removes the red bulb in the traffic light. Does it make it possible to go?

What if you take your foot off the break? Does that does make it possible for you to go? Probably not, unless of course you are on a hill and you could then go either forwards or backwards, depending on the hill. Either way, if you do move you are not influencing the direction you are going – the hill is.

And what if the car in front of you moves, does that make it possible for you to move too? Again no. So what will make it possible for you to go? Not the same things that cause you to stop, that's for sure.

What causes us to stop?	What causes us to start?
A red light showing on the traffic lights	A green light
Your foot on the break	A foot on the accelerator
The car in front	A clear road ahead

The things that cause you to stop at the junction are not the same things that cause you to start. The same is true in your sales interaction with the IT manager. He has told you the things that will stop him from buying your product because you asked him. The response you got was directly related to the question you asked. He hasn't told you the things that would make it possible for him to buy from you because you haven't asked him. Your question was inactive and therefore unproductive. You need to ask a different question.

Questions that make the sales process go (active questioning)

These questions are simply the inverse of the inactive questions we described above. Rather than asking the customer what would stop them from buying your product and service you ask them what they would need in order to consider purchasing your product or service. It focuses the customer's attention and your attention on the potential to do business, not on what stops the potential to do business. Productive? In our experience it's one of the most productive questions that any sales person can use. It quickly gets to the heart of what's valuable to the customer and gives you their real needs and desires so you can work with the customer rather than trying to put fires out. And what of the smart alec customer who, after asking him, 'What would need to happen in order for you buy our product?' replies with a curt 'Make it free!'? Well it could happen, but situations like this are few and far between. And for every situation when this occurs there will be a hundred where you'll actually go in a useful direction with the customer and begin to establish what truly will be valuable to them.

Maintaining the relationship

Clearly your ability to establish what's going to be valuable to the customer is dependent on asking productive questions that maintain the relationship and move the selling process forward. It's also dependent on your ability to create and maintain a valuable relationship with the customer through liking and listening. You also need to recognize that listening and liking isn't a one-off event. It is not a 'tick the box' done-that-bit-thank-you-very-much activity that you do at the start of a customer interaction and forget about it when it comes to the nitty gritty of asking questions. You need to maintain the relationship throughout and, whilst it's important that you've prepared good productive questions to find out what's important to your customer, it's crucial that the way you ask those questions doesn't have a detrimental effect on the relationship you have worked so hard to create. In simple terms you don't want to start interrogating your customers.

John Hughes' 1989 film *Uncle Buck* starred John Candy as the lovable uncle looking after his nephew and two nieces while their parents are out of town. In one classic scene in the kitchen over breakfast the nephew, played by Macalay Culkin, started to ask his uncle a few questions about what he did in his life:

Where do you live?

Do you have a house or an apartment?

Do you own or rent?

Are you married?

Ever been?

Ever want to be?

What's you job?

Do you wanna job?

Why?

Why?

And so it went on until the point when John Candy asks his nephew:

'What's your record for consecutive questions asked?' to which the reply came, **'38'**.

'That's pretty impressive', remarks the uncle.

'Well I'm a kid, that's my job', states the nephew.

Clearly the film demonstrates in a comical manner the inquisitiveness of a child, but there could also be a point to be made about how sales people might also approach the task of asking questions of customers. By simply running through a list, question after question, regardless of how productive those questions are, you can risk simply interrogating customers to the point where everything you do is counter-productive. What is needed is a way of incorporating your well-prepared and productive questions into an environment where a valuable customer relationship is maintained. How do you do it? Well if you consider that asking questions requires you to *take* information from the customer, to redress the balance you should *give* some information back to them.

Before asking a question it's often helpful to prepare your customer by giving them some information first as it can help to break the potential interrogational approach. For example, if you need to find out how much a potential customer has budgeted to spend on a particular product or service, what they'll be using it for and what kind of things are important to them, you could take a leaf out of the inquisitive six-year-old's book and just ask them almost in a military fashion:

How much have you got to spend?

What do you need it for?

What's important to you?

Alternatively you could apply a more 'consultative' approach by using the questioning and understanding cycle illustrated below.

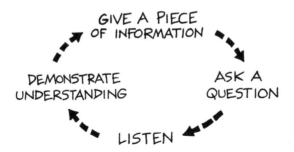

First you give a piece of information or make a statement connected to what you're going to ask. Next you ask your productive question. Then, taking your cue from the liking and listening principle, you listen to what the customer has said and then 'parrotphrase' it back using the customer's own words to demonstrate you have heard and understood them. Finally you wait for a typical response from a customer who has been understood: 'yes.'

Here's the example again in action. Let's assume the product is a hi-fi system.

SALES PERSON *(giving a piece of information)* 'There are actually quite a few different types of these products available now and they cover a wide range of prices.'

(asking a question) 'What kind of price do you have in mind?'

CUSTOMER 'There are a lot of products. It's almost overwhelming. I don't know, I guess about £300 I suppose.'

SALESPERSON *(listening and demonstrating understanding by repeating back)* 'It can be overwhelming but you can get a nice one for around . . . £300 you say?'

CUSTOMER 'Yes.'

SALES PERSON *(giving a piece of information)* 'I have smaller hi-fi at home which I use for connecting up to my PC.'

(asking a question) 'What are you going to be mainly using it for?'

CUSTOMER 'Well I have a digital TV and I want to connect the hi-fi up to get a better sound quality. And I also play a lot of CDs.'

SALES PERSON *(listening and demonstrating understanding by repeating back)* 'OK so as well as playing CDs you'd like to connect it up to your digital TV.'

CUSTOMER 'Yep!'

SALES PERSON *(giving a piece of information)* 'Lots of people have different ideas about what the best hi-fi for them is. Do you have any particular things that are going to be important to you?'

CUSTOMER *(asking a question)* 'Well I certainly don't want anything big and cumbersome. My TV takes up most of the space in the sitting room already and it needs to be easy to operate.'

SALES PERSON *(listening and demonstrating understanding by repeating back)* 'OK. Not too big then and one that's easy to operate. I think we have a couple of products that will fit the bill nicely.'

And so on and so on. The questioning and understanding cycle approach helps you to keep the sales process moving forward and maintain a valuable relationship with the customer in a very succinct and effective manner.

Why is it so effective? Because you do this anyway in your everyday life. When you come home from work at night and talk about the day's events with your family or friends you give them some information about your day and ask them about theirs. When you chat to friends on the telephone, conversations tend to be mixture of asking questions, giving information, listening and understanding. The same is true when you are in the pub with your mates or when you go out to dinner. It is a natural part of human interaction that sometimes gets forgotten when you start selling to people and fail to remember that you are still human and dealing with others who are also human. It's akin to having an invisible suit that you put on in the morning that suddenly changes you from being a normal human being into 'the sales person'. It doesn't have to be that way. By operating in a way that creates and maintains valuable customer relationships and productively gets to the heart of what's important and valuable to the customer you prepare the ground nicely for the next stage of the Effective Selling Principles. That, of course, is actually selling the product, or what we term 'Giving 'em what they want!'

Chapter 2 Establishing what is valuable to the customer (Being productive)

The questions you ask have an effect upon where a customer places their attention and therefore influence the responses you obtain. As a sales person you have to deal with those responses to progress the sale.

Questions are often characterized as being 'open' (in that they generate more substantial answers). 'Closed' (where they typically generate answers of just a word or two), for example, 'yes' and 'no'. However, it's more useful to consider the questions you ask as productive or un-productive.

A productive question:

- moves the selling process forward towards a useful outcome for both the customer and the sales person/company
- at least maintains or ideally enhances the relationship with the customer.

The questions that you ask will have an effect upon the relationship you have with your customers and your relationship with the customer will have an effect upon the questions you can ask.

You can avoid the possibility of interrogating your customers by using the questioning and understanding cycle.

Remember: Would you rather be right or would you rather be effective?

Creating a well-formed
sales goal

Creating and maintaining
a valuable customer relationship

Establishing what is valuable
to the customer

**Providing what is valuable to
the customer**

Gaining a commitment
to action

Providing what is valuable to the customer

(Giving 'em what they want)

Silence isn't golden, it's brown. A silent customer leaves us well and truly in the proverbial brown stuff.

One of the most enjoyable moments in selling[1] is when a customer asks *you* a question. It occurs a fair amount as it happens, especially if you get the 'liking and listening' and the 'being productive' principles about right. A customer who asks you questions is generally a good sign and at the very least it shows you that they are still awake!

There are other reasons why the idea of a customer asking you questions is generally productive. It could be that they require some more information, need to get clarification on a specific point you have made or sometimes they might even ask if they could buy something from you now (this is best of all). Assumptions are often dangerous, but whatever the reason for a customer asking a sales person a question there's one assumption that it's probably not that risky for you to make: Immediately after a customer asks you a question they are more likely to be listening than at any other time during the selling process. In situations like these then, you generally have a customer who is attentive to what you are going to say next and who is listening to you. In the same way that you've been careful to get across a clear message about the importance of listening and demonstrating understanding, it's important that you, too, have a way of knowing that your customer is ready to listen to what you have to say to them.

After all, if your customers aren't listening you may as well not be there.

The principles of providing what is valuable to the customer by presenting your product and services and then generating a commitment to buy from that customer are, in actual fact, the easiest elements of any sale providing you productively get to the heart of what's important to the customer.

---

1. Although we run a training company nothing actually gets trained until it gets sold. When people ask us what we do for a living we tell them that we are sales people – some people may not think it's cool to work in sales but we are proud of the fact. As Barry Gibbons, the former CEO of Burger King, says 'being cool ain't necessarily the same as being profitable'.

But how often do your sales calls fall on deaf ears? And what causes this to happen? Generally it's a function of the fact that you either haven't spent enough time establishing what's going to be valuable to the customer and demonstrating that you understand what's valuable and important to them or you simply have not done an effective enough job.

So, at what point do you know that you've been effective in establishing what's going to be valuable to the customer? What are the signs that you are looking or listening out for? And when's the best time to begin to present to your customer some ideas and options about how your products or services can provide that value? The answer, perhaps surprisingly, is a relatively straightforward one.

The best time to present your product or service to the customer is when they ask you to.

You know that you yourself are generally more likely to be listening to information that's given to you by someone else if you've requested it, and the same is true of your customers. But before we look at how you present information about your products or services, let's first briefly examine the cost of not having an attentive customer.

A solution looking for a problem?

How many times have you been in situations where a sales person starts 'selling' to you and you just shut down because you either have no interest in what they are saying or, due to the fact that they have either not listened to your needs or, worse still, never bothered to find out, just talk at you?

> How many times have you been in situations where a sales person starts 'selling' to you and you just shut down because you have no interest in what they are saying?

It is an experience that as customers we all have time and time and time again. Sales people presenting their products to us without finding out if we have a need. Companies focused on delivering messages or pushing particular product and service lines because that's their agenda rather than the agenda of their customers. Sometimes these things happen not because of anything sinister. Often they're the result of being too exuberant, they just get carried away. You might have such a belief in your product that it becomes unproductive when you start approaching customers. You think your product is the best thing since sliced bread[1] and you therefore feel the need to go out and 'tell' anybody[2] or anything[3] about it.

There is an adage in selling that says that customers tend to look for solutions to problems they have or improvements they wish to make. A family with rocketing utility bills (aka a problem) might look to companies who can help them make energy efficiencies and savings (aka solutions). These solutions might include switching to a more cost-effective utility company, insulating their house better or even moving house. A fast-growing business is operating from a number of outlets or offices in different towns or cities across the country might not have the best communication links between their sites (aka a problem) and seek options (solutions) for improving communications links.

But what about situations when the customer doesn't perhaps realize they have a problem? Maybe the customer is happy with their current circumstances and is not aware that there are newer, better or improved alternatives. Perhaps they don't see a need for your product or service – maybe their needs are already being met by what they are currently doing. What can you, as a sales person, do in these situations? Well, there's one thing that you certainly shouldn't do – and that's start to look for problems that *you think* a customer has! A kind of 'solution looking for a problem' if you like. This will only serve to create the potential for battle positions described previously.

'You need our product!'

'No I don't!'

Better that you establish what your customers find valuable and sell to what they have told you rather than sell to what you have told them. Approaching selling in this way creates a greater likelihood that a customer will ask you how you can help them. They literally ask you for ideas, options and solutions. It's like they are asking you to sell to them. It's like you're making it easy for them to buy from you. Sold!

---

1. Out of interest, what was the best thing before sliced bread?
2. Defined as having a pulse.
3. Defined as not having a pulse.

But what happens if a customer doesn't ask you to present to them your product or service? What are the options to you then? Well, following our cue from the whole theme of this book, you should seek the simple answer. And the simple answer in this case is that you ask them if you can present your product or service to them.

'So what you've told me is that as well as being able to connect the new hi-fi that you buy to your digital TV and play CDs you want something that costs around £300. Can I take you through some of the hi-fis we have that fit the bill?'

In this situation, where the customer has not asked you for a solution, you should ask them if they are ready to have one. You don't assume that it's time for you to give them your sales pitch – you simply ask them if they want to hear it or not. What are the potential responses from the customer? Well there are really only two. They could say 'yes' and they could say 'no'. If they say 'yes' then you're ready to move on. If they say 'no' then it's a signal that you're not yet ready to present your solution and you need to go back a stage and establish some more information about what the customer finds valuable. It's a simple reality check but one that's often missed in sales because you're either too focused on selling to the customer rather than on making it easier for the customer to buy from you. Or you might just be afraid of the customer saying no to you and sell to them anyway in the hope that you can convince them or change their mind with enthusiasm (or desperation) alone. But which is worse? A customer who tells you that they're not yet ready to buy because you haven't yet got a true and accurate picture of what they want or, a situation where your presentation falls on deaf ears. Feedback? or just wasting time, money and effort? Being right or being productive? A simple choice really.

Providing what is valuable to the customer

So you're at the point where the customer says OK so what are the options available, what can your product, service and company do for me? Or at the very least you're at the point where you have asked the customer if they're ready to hear what you have to say and they have replied in the positive.

What do you, the sales person, do?

The first thing you should do, at first glance, appears to be rather unproductive. In fact it appears to break every rule in the book. What we suggest you do just prior to presenting your product or service is that you *actually admit a weakness or drawback* about it.

What we suggest you do just prior to presenting your product or service is that you *actually admit a weakness or drawback* about it.

What can the benefit of such a strange strategy be? After all you're at the point of the sale where the customer has either asked you to provide some ideas about a solution or you've asked them if you can present to them. The customer is attentive. The customer is listening. The customer is ready to hear every word and the first thing we say to them is actually detrimental to the very thing you want to achieve. Attaining a successful sale. 'Sorry guys,' we hear you cry, 'you've lost it.'

But let's look a little closer at this.

The apparent 'daftness' of this idea is one that's used with great success by the brewing industry and specifically Stella Artois – the 'reassuringly expensive' beer. If you were with us in Chapter 2, you'll have learnt that we're occasional 'consumers' of the Belgian yellow stuff. One thing we didn't let you in on was our love of, and apparent ability to, complain when companies, let's say, take the yellow stuff out of us.[1] But there's one thing about Stella Artois that we've never complained or commented about and that's the fact that *it actually is more expensive*. Another example of this 'daftness' comes from the world of car hire and rentals where Avis is happy to admit that they are not the number-one car-hire and rental company in the world. In fact they openly admit: 'We're number two – so we try harder for you.'

Some of us will, at some point in our lives, have been on holiday to a destination that required us to have the dreaded but necessary 'holiday jab'.

---

1. The best and most recent example of a company who takes the 'yellow stuff' being the Royal Mail's telephone 'helpline' which, in its wisdom, has now decided to charge Johnny Customer 50 pence a minute if we want to know someone's postcode (read ZIP in the US). The Royal Mail invented postcodes to make their lives easier and now they charge us for the privilege. It actually costs them more money to deliver items without postcodes, so guess what we *don't* do anymore? At least when they called themselves Consignia they were telling us what they were doing.

Even if you haven't, when you were young you would have had a number of vaccinations to protect you from potentially dangerous illnesses and infections. A vaccine works primarily by introducing a weakened from of a particular illness into your body. Your body recognizes this illness and produces antibodies so that if you're at risk of this illness at a future date you have the defences to fight off the risk. This works in much the same way as you can protect yourself from a variety of 'problems' by doing something similar in sales. By introducing a potential weakness or drawback to your product or service it makes it less likely for a customer to actually bring up this drawback or weakness at future point in the sales process. Now we're not advocating that you create potential issues for yourselves by bringing up major drawbacks or stumbling blocks[1] that would prohibit a sale. We are talking about using maybe a well-known or potentially 'easily dealt with' weakness.

As Stella Artois and Avis have found to their benefit, admitting a drawback can have the effect of inoculating us against a potential issue that would be possibly more difficult to deal with further on in the sales process. But there's an even more beneficial reason for using this 'daft' idea of admitting a weakness and it has much to do with the very thing you say next. It's actually perceived to be more believable. How can this be? Well let's consider the facts.

Admitting a small weakness about your product or service sends a message to the customer, at a point when they're most likely to be listening to you, that you're honest and trustworthy – the very ingredients that will maintain the valuable relationship you have created. After all aren't there a lot of customers who believe that sales people are supposed to say whatever's necessary to coerce their way into getting a sale?

'Here's a refreshing approach,' thinks the customer, 'a sales person admitting where there are drawbacks to their product. Maybe this sales person is different. Maybe they do speak the truth. Maybe they do have my best interests at heart. Maybe I should listen very carefully to what they say next.'

---

1. Hopefully you shouldn't have too many.

Let's take an example of a sales person selling hi-fi equipment. The sales person could quite conceivably admit that *'this particular stereo system might lose a little sound clarity at very high volumes'* and then go on to point out two or three very important benefits that make this apparent weakness appear almost unimportant, at the same time sending a signal to the customer that we will present a very fair and honest case for the product in question.

Sold!

So that's it then, is it? Just admit a small weakness about your product or service happy in the knowledge that whatever you say next will literally have the customer begging to buy your product. Well, not quite. There's just one final thing you need to do. You need to provide your product or service information to the customer in a way that makes it easy for them to say 'yes' to you. How do you do this? Well again you take the cue from the customer, as often they will tell you how they like to buy. As with every other principle of effective selling we have spoken about thus far, you need to have your eyes and ears open and ready for when it happens.

A few weeks ago, in an activity we justified to ourselves as 'research', we went shopping. We quickly came to the conclusion that there are too many missed sales opportunities – even when the sales person had done all the hard work. The example that sticks in our mind the clearest was when we went to 'buy' a laptop computer. It's only fair to point that we were genuinely looking for a laptop and were willing to buy one that day. One chap did a great job on us. After asking us a few productive and relevant questions about what we needed he was ready to get down to the presentation.

'There are few that fit the bill as it happens', our sales person happily informed us.

'Excellent, can we try a few out then, please?'

'Sure, take a look at these', as he pointed to a very glossy brochure of three potentially suitable laptop computers.

He certainly knew his stuff. On a roll and with us as his captive audience he demonstrated with the utmost competence why two of the three computers in particular would be especially suitable to our needs.

Whilst we would like to honour this young man for the amount of time he had clearly spent gaining a substantial amount of information about the products he was selling and for being so enthusiastic there was one thing that he failed to appreciate. We didn't want him to show us a brochure and tell us what computers suited our needs. We wanted to *try them out!*

A question that we often ask sales representatives is how they chose their company cars. Like many sales representatives their company provided them all with a company car of their choice from a list of those available. What was really interesting about the subsequent discussion was not the fact that there were many different ways that the people made a decision about what car they would choose, anyone could have predicted that. No, what was odd was the fact that the conversations that followed were primarily about how strange the colleagues were who didn't make decisions in the same way as them.

Some people wouldn't even go near a car showroom until they had studied the specifications in the product brochure. Others couldn't care less what the brochure looked like, they wanted to know what their friends and family thought. One woman was, in fact, about to choose her new car. 'Have you made a decision yet?' we asked. 'Well sort of', she replied. Everyone's quizzical looks prompted her to explain further.

'I own a dog and therefore I need an estate car. My current car is perfect, it is the ideal size and there's plenty of room in the back to accommodate my dog and his basket. So I am going to buy the exact same car again.'

'So you've made a decision then', remarked a colleague.

'Well no. I still have to go down to the showroom and put my dog and his basket in the new car to see for myself that it all fits.'

'But it's the same car. What if you saw the brochure and that confirmed that the sizes were the same. Would that help?'

'No.'

'What if someone told you they had an even bigger dog and dog basket and theirs fitted OK. Would you be able to choose then?'

'No. I have to see for myself. Nothing else will do. I know it sounds stupid but that's just the way it is.'

And she's right. It's just the way it is. As sales people you need to figure out how the customer wants presented to them what you have established as being valuable to them. And there is generally only a few ways that this works.

We've all been given five senses and five tools to use them. We also have a whole dialect that we use to describe what we senses we are using.

'Show, tell and experience'

If someone says, 'show me some information about that' they are asking you to show them some more information. They are not asking for you to tell them something. They are not asking for a demonstration. They're asking for you to show them some more information. Our sales representative friend needed to 'see for her own eyes' that her dog and her dog's basket fitted in her new car. It might sound irrational to others but to her it was the decision factor. If you are selling a car to this woman you need to know that and then make it possible for her to see it 'with her own eyes'.

> **If a customer says that they want to talk to someone about your product, they are telling you that they want to talk to someone (and probably not you!)**

Our friend in the computer store, whilst knowledgeable and very professional, didn't recognize that we needed to try a computer out, not hear about how great it is.

Clearly when you are providing what is going to be valuable to the customer it should include not only the information that you have established as being valuable to them by the productive questions you asked. You should also present that information to them in a way that the customer finds most valuable. And how do you know what that will be? Well, as with pretty much everything else we have talked about, the answer is to listen to the clues the customer gives you and/or to ask them.

If a customer says to us, 'I'd like to hear some more about that', then you need to *tell* them.

If a customer says they want to 'get a better feel' for your product, then you need to make it possible for them to get that experience by setting up a trial of your product and/or letting them have a go at using it.

If a customer says that they want to talk to someone about your product, they are telling you that they want to talk to someone (and probably not you!) so you need to help that conversation take place.

There's nothing definite about selling as it involves one individual communicating with another and therefore we can only talk about principles and common themes. However there's one thing that's pretty much definite. In any sales scenario where a customer communicates that something has to happen before they can move towards a commitment to buying our product or service then it's pretty much going to have to happen. Period.

Whilst our world is made up of millions and millions of individuals interacting with millions and millions of others, we all still have only five ways of taking in information. This makes your life a little easier because as long as you have the chance to present information in one of these ways, you can be well prepared for most selling situations. And in fact, of the five ways of presenting (showing, telling, touching (experience), smelling and tasting) it's usually the show, tell and experience means that most people prefer.

As a sales person you therefore need to listen to what's important to the customer in terms of how they would like information presented to them, and then present it. This will require some forward-planning in terms of what materials, demonstrations and information you will need to prepare in advance or have with you when you are selling. But it's time well invested. It can and will make the difference between going from customer to customer selling to them rather than making it easier for those customers to buy from you.

**Chapter 3 Providing what is valuable to the customer
(giving 'em what they want)**

The best time to present your product or service proposal is when the customer asks you to. That way you can be sure they are attentive and listening to you.

If the customer doesn't ask then you should prompt them by asking if it's OK to proceed.

Admitting a small weakness or drawback to your proposal not only makes your proposal more credible, it can also help to alleviate any potential customer objections that might arise.

Show, tell and experience

Ask the customer how they would like to have your product or service presented to them. We all use our senses to take on board information and everyone has their own preferences. The customer might prefer to be shown the product, told about it or may like to experience it (and sometimes a customer will want a combination or all three).

Use the same words and phrases that the customer used when you were using productive questions to find out what was valuable to them.

Have all your materials, product information, samples and literature to hand so that you have the resources required to present in a way that suits the customer.

Remember, when you are done you are done. Present what is important and valuable to the customer – often that means you don't have to tell them everything. Don't talk yourself out of a sale.

Creating a well-formed
sales goal

Creating and maintaining
a valuable customer relationship

Establishing what is valuable
to the customer

Providing what is valuable to
the customer

**Gaining a commitment
to action**

Gaining a commitment to action

(Sold!)

One of the most common questions we're asked is what is the best way to close a sale. By closing a sale what we think people mean is how do we get the customer to say 'yes', to say, 'I'm ready to buy from you,' to say 'Where do I sign?' We've lost count of the number of times that sales managers, team leaders and sales directors have asked if we can come and help their sales teams and sales people develop their closing skills.

And it's because the issue of closing more sales is the one in the selling process that is most often talked about and demanded by the sales hierarchy that we have decided, in fact, to make this the shortest and not the longest of our chapters.

The reason is a simple one. We think that too much attention is placed on a topic that in essence is simple and straightforward. Think about it. If you haven't got the customer in a state where they are ready to buy your product, it's a symptom of what happened before, not what technique you use next to attempt to close the sale. You can ask as many closing questions as you like. It ain't gonna make a ha'penny worth of difference. If a customer says no to you then it's more likely to be due to the fact that you either have a customer who was unlikely to buy anyway (see the Introduction) or the sales process went awry some time before. Perhaps you didn't establish the relationship as best you could. Maybe you weren't productive enough when establishing what was valuable to your customer or maybe the presentation of your product didn't serve to really give the customer what they really wanted.

Closing. Who the hell needs closed customers?

Surely you want customers who make long-term commitments to your products, your services, your brands, your company and you? Surely that's the aspiration of every sales person as it makes life so much easier. Let's take an example. Here's a rather well-known brand that you may have heard of.

Coca-Cola is currently[1] the world's most recognized brand. A famous icon in pretty much every country in the world, as a brand and a product it has it all. Awareness, presence and a customer and consumer base so loyal that when they replaced Coca-Cola with New Coke in the 1980s there was almost a military coup. But let's ask ourselves a question. Did it achieve this overnight? Did the Coca-Cola Company one day just decide that it was going to be the greatest and most recognized brand in the world? Of course not. It was hard work with many years of planning, investment and careful nurturing. And it continues today – it cannot afford to rest on its laurels, especially in a global environment of increasing competition and more demanding customers and consumers. The interesting thing about Coca-Cola (or any other successful brand you care to name) is that the success started with a customer buying a bottle . . . can . . . box . . . carton . . . or whatever of the stuff.

So what has Coca-Cola and branding have to do with selling and closing and getting commitments from customers? Surely we're not suggesting that sales people be like brands? Actually that's exactly what we're suggesting. Let's look again at Coca-Cola. When it sold its product to a customer for the first time, did it close that customer and then move on to the next potential customer, and the next, and so on, simply closing each and

---

1. And has been for what seems like for ever.

every customer that it came into contact with? Or did they do something different? Did they take each customer and work out how they could become more and more committed to using more and more Coca-Cola in the future? Did they think about how that one-time customer could become a lifetime customer?

You betcha! Closing. Who the hell needs closed customers?

But hold on a moment. Coca-Cola is a product that thrives on continued use. Its very growth comes from increasing both the numbers of customers that consume it and the amount they consume. How about sales people that sell in environments where a customer will only buy a product from them once? Surely they are not like Coca-Cola? Well actually the analogy still holds true. There are people all over the world who drink Coca-Cola because it's Coca-Cola and here's the clue for those of you who sell in one-time environments.

Having an objective of selling a product or service to a customer is actually inefficient and can make selling more difficult for you in the future. Seeing each customer as a one-off sale won't get you into the position of being seen as trusted adviser or friend in the same way as Coca-Cola is seen. Surely it's better to have an objective that not only results in a successful buying experience for the customer but also actually gets the customer to commit to generating more customers for you by becoming a sales person too. On your behalf! For your product and your service. Now that's what *we would* call a commitment to action. Satisfied customers making long-term commitments to use your products, your store or your service time and time again and also telling their friends, families and colleagues to do the same. And even if they are only able to purchase your product once what if they were to make a commitment to tell other potential customers about you and how good it is to do business with you.

Having an objective of selling a product or service to a customer is actually inefficient and can make selling more difficult for you in the future.

We know a retailer whose outlets sold, among other electrical items, televisions and videos. One particular store would typically sell 10–12 televisions on a Saturday. The store's area manager would often offer the incentive of a prize to the sales person who sold the most televisions during a Saturday's trading. Everyone in the store got into the incentive and would look to outperform their colleagues to win that week's prize. Great idea you would think. Sell more products, create a buzz in the working environment and listen to the ringing of the tills. Great idea – everyone's happy – everything is going swimmingly. Or is it? Well possibly not. The area manager was incentivizing his team to sell televisions today and as a result that was what his team was focused on. Sell televisions today and we'll worry about tomorrow, tomorrow. The very focus on closing today's sales limited their ability to help more customers buy more products in the future. Why? Because the sales team was not focused on what will make today's customer a repeat customer tomorrow. Or what will make today's customer recommend another potential customer for tomorrow. What the area manager might be advised to consider in future incentives is how many televisions can his team sell to customers who have been recommended by another customer. That sort of approach could mean the difference between selling 10–12 televisions a week and selling, let's say 20.

Today's sale is tomorrow's history and the thing about history is it doesn't change. A customer who you close today is a customer who could be closed tomorrow. A committed customer today could still be a committed customer tomorrow and that's what you're looking to generate. A customer that not only makes a commitment to buy from you today but also one that, through their commitment to you, your products, your services and your company will return and buy tomorrow.

And hopefully when they come back they bring a few friends with them too!

It seems therefore that rather than attempting to close a sale you should focus on ways that you can help a customer to make a longer-term commitment. Generating that commitment will ensure that you have an advocate as a customer. A customer that not only enjoys and finds it easy to buy from you but one who also recommends your products and services to others.

Do such customers exist? Absolutely and although you all probably have them, there's certainly no harm in having a few more.

Under these circumstances will a customer actually make such a commitment? The answer is in the subjects that we've already discussed. A customer is most likely to make a commitment when you've provided something of value to them and the way to do that is to establish a relationship and ask productive questions that get to the heart of their wants and needs.

And finally, when a customer does make a commitment what do you, the sales person, need to do to ensure that it is lived up to? Well, here's where it gets very interesting. In transactional selling there's a clear sign when a customer makes a commitment because the next stage involves the customer either handing over cash, a cheque, a credit card or possibly signing some sort of order form. Fine if, like our friends in the example above, you are selling televisions. But what about the situations when you might have to sell to the same customer time and again. Or what of scenarios when, in order to sell your products and services, you might need to gain access to a number of different decision-makers in the same company or account?

Selling is one thing but getting a commitment for someone to act differently is often an entirely different animal.

How do you get a commitment to advance the process? And what if you are selling televisions. How do you get a commitment from a customer to tell others about your great products and service or get them to come and buy from you time and time again? Selling is one thing but getting a commitment for someone to act differently is often an entirely different animal.

Fortunately people have been asking this same question for years and years. And for good reasons too. You have experienced situations where people say they will do something and either do the opposite or never quite get round to doing what they have committed themselves to. It can be frustrating, especially in the world of sales where your urgency to sell to a customer is sometimes greater than the customer's urgency to buy.

Before we seek answers to what makes a customer commitment actually likely to be acted upon, let's review some actual real-life sales interactions. The following 'commitments' were made by real customers to real sales people in real selling situations. Judge for yourself which ones you believe are most likely to be valuable commitments.

Customer Commitment	A useful customer commitment?	
1. The customer agrees to write an e-mail to a colleague in another department to inform them of his support for your product.	☺ YES ☺ MAYBE ☹ NO	☐ ☐ ☐
2. The customer asks you to send them more information.	☺ YES ☺ MAYBE ☹ NO	☐ ☐ ☐
3. The sales person asks if the customer will bear their product in mind and the customer replies that they will.	☺ YES ☺ MAYBE ☹ NO	☐ ☐ ☐
4. The customer phones a friend or colleague while they are still with you to tell them how useful the time you have spent was.	☺ YES ☺ MAYBE ☹ NO	☐ ☐ ☐
5. The customer agrees to make a further appointment for you to see them with their manager to take things forward.	☺ YES ☺ MAYBE ☹ NO	☐ ☐ ☐
6. The customer takes your business card and agrees to call you in a week's time.	☺ YES ☺ MAYBE ☹ NO	☐ ☐ ☐
7. The customer has asked if you would take them and their team out for a meal next week to celebrate someone's leaving do.	☺ YES ☺ MAYBE ☹ NO	☐ ☐ ☐
8. The customer will tell their manager about your meeting and pass on your business card to them.	☺ YES ☺ MAYBE ☹ NO	☐ ☐ ☐
9. You write a follow-up e-mail to your customer informing them of what has been agreed.	☺ YES ☺ MAYBE ☹ NO	☐ ☐ ☐
10. The customer writes you a follow-up e-mail outlining what has been agreed between you.	☺ YES ☺ MAYBE ☹ NO	☐ ☐ ☐

So how did you do?

Let's take them in turn. Are they genuine commitments, maybes, or just lip service?

1. This could be a genuine commitment as it involves someone else in the company as well. Here you would try to be copied in on the e-mail so that you have a direct follow-up with the colleague.

2. No way. Generally this can often be a waste of money – for the company paying for the printing. This is feedback for the sales person that either the customer is not in a position to buy or is unhappy with what they are doing (for ways of dealing with this turn to the last chapter).

3. Nope. Easy for the customer to say they will bear it in mind. What will they bear in mind? No sale here, sorry.

4. Yes. This is productive. Again someone else other than the customer is involved.

5. Yes again. Someone else is involved (the boss in this case) and a follow-up action has been arranged.

6. You might spend a lot of time waiting for the phone to ring.

7. Maybe. On the plus side you get to see the whole of this customer's department. On the downside you might just be spending your entertainment budget. It might be worth asking for an agreement to purchase something before proceeding.

8. Maybe. Will they tell their manager now while you are still with them though? Asking that will give you a real feel for how genuine the commitment to move on is.

9. No. The sales person is making all the moves here. No commitment at all.

10. Yes, although you need to make sure that the sales process gets followed up quickly while it is fresh in their mind and yours.

So a quick look at ten genuine outcomes of ten genuine sales calls only three at best resulted in moving the sale forward to any degree. Clearly some clues to what makes a genuine customer commitment are needed. And as is the case with our principle of creating and maintaining a valuable customer relationship, the clues come from the world of social science.

According to Professor Robert Cialdini there are three ingredients that make the difference between a commitment of sorts and a genuine commitment that a customer is more likely to act upon. However, before we embark on what those three ingredients are, we need to just remind ourselves of one very important fact. As human beings we tend to want to remain consistent with thoughts, beliefs, opinions and values that we hold true to ourselves. Understanding what those thoughts, beliefs, opinions and values are can mean the difference between a successful commitment (sale) and not. It's therefore important to point out once again that the ability to successfully generate a commitment to buy comes from your ability to establish what is important. A commitment that's not aligned to what's important to the customer will turn out to be anything but a commitment. So what are the three ingredients that make up a genuine commitment?

Ownership of commitments

He who is complies against his will is still of the same opinion.

In organizations, families, governments and many other groups of people there are those who command and have authority and those who obey. Even though you might comply with someone who is more senior than you or who has a higher position in the hierarchy, they do not necessarily change your opinion about what you have been told to do. As a sales person you rarely have authority over a customer. You need to persuade and influence as opposed to tell. The commitments that are most likely to be acted upon are those that your customer suggests and therefore owns. Asking questions at the end of the sales process that provoke the customer into making owned commitments are more likely to result in sales success. All that simply telling and asking will generate is resistance and failure.

Action-based commitments

Professor Cialdini describes commitments that involve an action on the part of the person who makes the commitment as being more likely to be acted upon than those that require little or no action at all. In our real-life examples of earlier, the situations where the customer agreed to do something resulted in commitments where the sales process would move forward. Customers who sent e-mails to colleagues to progress the sale, perhaps set up meetings, or go away and source some specific information are all examples of the customer taking some kind of 'action'. It's these actions that will make a commitment more likely to be followed through. Conversely, situations where the sales person comes away at the end of a sales call with a thousand things to action for the customer only indicate the sales person's commitment to the customer. They don't indicate the customer's commitment to the sales person. Any commitment that you generate from a customer should have some form of activity that the customer will action. It's worth asking yourself, 'how committed is this customer?' if they refuse to be involved in taking the sale forward.

Public commitments

The more people who know about something the more it is likely to happen. In fact the more an individual publicly declares to others something that's important to them or an action they are going to take, the more committed that person becomes to the idea. A friend of ours, who a few years ago tried to give up smoking, demonstrated one of the best examples of a public commitment in action to us.

It wasn't the first time our friend had attempted to give up smoking and he had tried every way known to man, from will power alone to nicotine replacement patches, to those funny little pretend cigarettes. Each time he tried he was successful for maybe a few weeks but it wasn't long afterwards that he slipped back into the habit. That changed one day when he did one extra thing that he had failed to do in every other attempt to give up smoking. He told lots of people about the fact that he had now given up smoking. And he didn't just tell anyone. Our friend told people that he respected. The sorts of people that it would be painful to 'lose face' with. He made a public commitment and the moment he made that public commitment the image of himself changed. In every other attempt he was only letting himself down when he failed to successfully give up smoking. This time was different. If he failed this time he was letting not just himself down but others he respected too.

Every one of us has known situations where people will say they will do something and they never quite get round to it. Everyone, especially in the sales environment, has customers we can never quite get to commit to a course of action that either gets them to purchase our products and services or move the sale forward in some way. What the 'owned', 'active' and 'public' elements give you is a way of judging how committed a customer is. The world of social science tells us that when these three elements are present in a commitment that we generate from a customer, that commitment is more likely to be acted upon than one that doesn't have them present.

Like many companies selling business to business we're often asked by customers to write proposals. A lot of sales people would consider a customer asking for a proposal to be a 'buying signal'. Surely a customer that asks for a proposal is interested in your products and services? Clearly a customer asking for a proposal means you have a real opportunity of securing the business? We're not always so sure. And it's a problem that a lot of sales people struggle with as a lot of time and money can be invested in proposals that serve merely to get a sales person out of a customer's office or, worse still, give the customer a few pages of 'free ideas' that then get implemented by the customer themselves or another (often cheaper) supplier.

So how can the 'owned', 'active' and 'public' elements of a commitment serve you better when you are dealing with customers who demand proposals or more information? Well the obvious answer is to ask the customer whether they would work on the proposal with you. That's the sign of a genuine commitment as it's 'owned' and 'active' from the customer's perspective. Often a proposal has to be presented to others in a company. Having an insider who has actively taken part in the development of a proposal then discusses it with colleagues is also making a public commitment to the proposal. What a great way to generate business. Have the customer help you sell the product because they are actively involved in the process. They own the proposal as much as you do. Sold!

But what if a customer refuses to be involved in a proposal? What can you do then? Well the first thing might be to consider how genuinely committed the customer actually is to considering your product or service. If you consider that they are worth pursuing then what other commitments could the customer make that use one or all of the 'owned', 'active' and 'public' elements of a genuine commitment?

Perhaps they would arrange for you to talk to other decision-makers in the company. Maybe they would source some additional information that would make your proposal more specific to what they will consider to be valuable to them. Maybe they will allow you to present the proposal to the decision-makers rather than just post it to them and risk your hard work getting lost in the middle of a huge file of other proposals from other companies.

The same is true of repeat business. We have stressed on a number of occasions that today's sale is only tomorrow's history. You don't just want to sell a product today. You want those customers to make a commitment to being a customer tomorrow and ideally bring some more new customers back with them.

Chapter 4 Gaining a commitment to action
(Sold!)

Closing just focuses on an action today and, while that might be useful today, it doesn't necessarily equate to a committed customer of tomorrow.

Genuine commitments to action are those that contain the following three elements:

- Ownership – the customer must own the commitment. A coerced or forced action is not commitment, it is compliance and compliance is usually just a one-off affair.
- Action – commitments that require an action from the customer are more likely to be acted upon. Sales calls that result in the sales person having all the actions is a sales person who has made a commitment to the customer, not the other way round.
- Public – A genuine commitment is one that is made public. The more people that know about something the more likely the sale is to progress. Increasingly, especially when selling to businesses, there are more and more people involved in buying decisions. Make all your actions in an account public to everyone and get your customers to make their commitments to you public also.

The most likely commitment to a purchase is one that provides to the customer what you have established as valuable to them. The customer has declared (and therefore owns) their needs and desires. Aligning your product to what a customer has publicly declared as important is the way that you will make is easier to get a commitment from that customer.

Creating a well-formed
sales goal

Creating and maintaining
a valuable customer relationship

Establishing what is valuable
to the customer

Providing what is valuable to
the customer

Gaining a commitment
to action

Creating a well-formed sales goal

(Getting ready)

If, when you drop your toast, the buttered side always lands on the floor then prepare in advance and butter the other side.

You might be forgiven for wondering why the chapter on setting well-formed sales goals is the last in our presentation of the five principles of effective selling. Surely it makes more sense for it to be the first? If, for example, you were to go on a car journey it would make sense to look at a map and plan your route before you get into your vehicle? Well, that may be true, but planning your route presupposes that your vehicle is in good condition and you know how to drive it. The same is true in sales. Having a well-formed sales goal with a clear direction of what you want to achieve is fine but if you don't know how to achieve it then your sales goal is, in isolation, pretty useless.

It is for this reason that we won't focus too much on the rather well-known acronym for setting goals called SMART.[1]

We don't have anything against SMART objectives. In fact they make good sense in terms of describing *what* you should think about when formulating an objective but they don't tell you *how* to go about achieving the objective.

---

1. Specific Measured Action-based Realistic Timed.

There's also a reason why we've decided to talk about 'sales goals' rather than objectives and that's to direct your attention to formulating sales goals that have the sale as your primary focus. Your job is to sell and therefore your business goals should be measured in terms of the sales you generate.

Our previous chapters have described the 'how' part of the selling process:

Listen to the customer and find areas of similarity and liking, be productive in the way you establish what is valuable to them, give the customer what you have established as valuable and then get a commitment to action.

You merely need to review them briefly and then collate them with what you want to achieve and your sales goal is created. And here is the interesting thing. Thinking through and creating a well-formed sales goal in this way means you are literally creating an image of you conducting the sale before you come to do it for real.

Put simply, you are preparing yourself to make it easier for the customer to buy from you.

Clear goals are key to managing your success as a sales person and there are numerous studies that reinforce the fact. In one particular study a famous university tracked one group of their students who had written down clear, identifiable goals and outcomes that they desired and another group of students who hadn't written down or considered what they wanted to achieve. A few years later they compared the subsequent achievements of the two groups and the results were astounding. The students who had had clear goals mapped out and written down were worth some ten times more financially than the students who hadn't had goals. Now, while this study only used financial reward as its measure, it does give a clear indication as to the value of setting clear goals.

So how do goals and objectives work in the world of sales?

Well they help you create a map of what you want to achieve and then the Effective Selling Principles we've described give you the tools to prompt you *how* you're going to achieve your goal!

It seems simple, and after a while it is. But like most things the first few times take a little longer. However, we urge you to persevere as you will quickly become more and more proficient at creating well-formed sales goals and subsequently more skilled at helping your customers to buy from you.

So how do you create a well-formed sales goal? Well there are only a few pointers. Let's take each one in turn:

1. What do you want to achieve? (make it a positive outcome). The number of sales people who say what they don't want as their goal amazes us. They literally say things like, 'I'm going to see this customer because I don't want him to use any more of the competitor's product'. Well-formed goals are always stated in the positive and focus on what you can do, not what someone else is doing.

2. How will you know you have been successful in achieving your goal? What will be the signs?

   ● Think through how you will create and maintain a valuable customer relationship by *liking and listening*.

   ● Know what information you'll need in order to establish what is valuable to the customer and how you'll elicit that information by using *productive questions* that move both the sales process and the relationship forward.

   ● Consider the materials, brochures, demonstration items and any other resources you might need to provide what is valuable to the customer and thereby *give 'em what they want* before finally . . .

   ● Having a clear idea of how you will generate a commitment to action and get the customer to either *buy* or progress the sale in a favourable way.

   Incorporate signposts into your goals so that if what you're doing isn't working you know you need to do something else instead.

   If you know what you want you should have a clear vision of what the successful outcome will look like.

   If during your progress towards that sales goal you find things are not quite working out then you will need to change what you are doing.

It's the old car journey analogy we mentioned at the beginning of the chapter. If you are going to drive from London to Leeds you will see signposts along the way that let you know you are going in the right direction. You can incorporate signposts into the goals you set for your customer interactions in just the same way. What will be the signs that will let you know the sale is progressing and what will you do if the sales process goes a little off-piste?

3. Is your goal personal or competitive? Let's explain. If your goal is to be in the top 10 per cent of the sales team you're relying on 90 per cent of the sales team performing less well than you. This is something you have no control over. However, if you know what you need to do to be in the top 10 per cent then this can be translated into a personal goal. You now have control. You should always have control over your sales goals. It's uncomfortable because there's no one else that can take the blame if it goes awry but it's when you achieve them you can be proud in the knowledge that your success is down to your own performance.

4. Finally if, for whatever reason, you don't get to achieve your sales goal, what could you achieve that would be positive? This is known as your fallback or second position. Always aim to build a fallback into your goals.

If the customer doesn't buy today would they commit to something that takes the sales process forward? Fallbacks can be a powerful way of staying motivated on days when things don't go so well. To have some positive outcome or result from every sales interaction your conduct keeps you going when others fall by the wayside.

So how often do you create and set sales goals and how well do you perform against them? How motivated are you to create some specific sales goals and perform to your best ability?

You can find out the answers by completing the following goal-setting questionnaire.

Place a tick in the appropriate box as shown in the first example question. There are no right or wrong answers. Once you have completed all 30 you can score your answers with the scorecard on page 86. Take your time and answer each question honestly. The results that the questionnaire generates will only be as accurate as the answers that you give.

Goal-setting questionnaire

	Strongly agree	Agree	Agree to some extent	Disagree	Strongly disagree
Example: I always set clear and measurable goals.		✓			
1. Invariably the goal that I am working towards is one that I genuinely want to achieve.					
2. I prefer to be given goals or objectives that I need to achieve.					
3. It's not whether I finish top or bottom that matters; it's the fact that I have improved my performance overall.					
4. I tend to record or log my goals in some way and revisit them regularly.					
5. The goals that I strive to achieve are set by me personally.					
6. The prospect of suffering some form of rebuke is a powerful motivator for me to reach my objectives.					
7. My primary goal is always to be among the top performers in my peer group.					
8. As long as I have a rough idea of what's needed I invariably get there.					
9. I take the time to think through my goals and create a mental picture of me achieving them.					

10.	I have no control over others so I just concentrate on what I can do to achieve my goals.									
11.	I like the idea of being recognized for a good performance.									
12.	I set very challenging yet realistic goals.									
13.	I always strive to compete at the highest level even if an activity is new to me.									
14.	I carefully think through and know what successfully achieving my goal will be like.									
15.	I have been known to set goals that I think others want me to achieve.									
16.	I like the idea of setting one goal and achieving it before moving on to the next one.									
17.	I have sometimes been guilty of carrying out a task or activity for fear of what will happen if I don't.									
18.	The idea of being considered the best performer by my peers is exciting to me.									
19.	I often carry out tasks and activities that by personal choice I personally would not do.									
20.	The goals I have and strive to achieve I do for me personally.									
21.	The appeal of being recognized and rewarded is a powerful motivator to me.									
22.	I know what I don't want and I make surel set goals for avoiding it.									

Goal-setting questionnaire
continued

	Strongly agree	Agree	Agree to some extent	Disagree	Strongly disagree
23. I would rather be given a task or activity with clearly defined outcomes by a manager or superior.					
24. Beating others is my primary goal.					
25. I am clear about the things I want in my life and have a clear plan of how to achieve them.					
26. As long as I am performing well when compared to others then I feel OK.					
27. Anything less than a top performance is very demotivating to me.					
28. I often review where I am, where I am going and make changes where necessary.					
29. I am often more motivated to perform if there is a risk of me getting into trouble if I don't.					
30. Feeling like I'm No. 1. That's the feeling I'm looking to achieve in m goals.					

Your Scores

Circle the score for each of your answers. For example, if you answered 'Disagree' for Question 1 then you would score 2 as in the example below. Once you've circled the scores for each of the questions transfer them to the scoring box and add up the totals for each category. Once you have a total for each category you can plot your results on the grid and read about your profile.

Goal-setting scorecard

	Strongly agree	Agree	Agree to some extent	Disagree	Strongly disagree
EXAMPLE					
Question 1	5	4	3	②	1
Question 1	5	4	3	2	1
Question 2	1	2	3	4	5
Question 3	5	4	3	2	1
Question 4	5	4	3	2	1
Question 5	5	4	3	2	1
Question 6	1	2	3	4	5
Question 7	1	2	3	4	5
Question 8	1	2	3	4	5
Question 9	5	4	3	2	1
Question 10	5	4	3	2	1
Question 11	5	4	3	2	1
Question 12	5	4	3	2	1

▶

Goal-setting score card continued	Strongly agree	Agree	Agree to some extent	Disagree	Strongly disagree
Question 13	5	4	3	2	1
Question 14	5	4	3	2	1
Question 15	1	2	3	4	5
Question 16	1	2	3	4	5
Question 17	1	2	3	4	5
Question 18	1	2	3	4	5
Question 19	1	2	3	4	5
Question 20	5	4	3	2	1
Question 21	5	4	3	2	1
Question 22	1	2	3	4	5
Question 23	1	2	3	4	5
Question 24	1	2	3	4	5
Question 25	5	4	3	2	1
Question 26	1	2	3	4	5
Question 27	1	2	3	4	5
Question 28	5	4	3	2	1
Question 29	1	2	3	4	5
Question 30	5	4	3	2	1

Now transfer your scores from the score card to the scoring box and then add up your scores to come up with column totals.

Scoring box

Goal-setting		Internal/ external		Performance/ competitiveness		Motivation	
Question number	Your score	Question number	Your score	Question number	Your score	Question number	Your score
4		1		3		6	
8				7			
9		2					
12		5				11	
13		15		10		17	
14		19					
16				18		21	
22				24		29	
25		20		26			
28		23		27		30	
Total column score		Total column score		Total column score		Total column score	

Transfer your scores to the corresponding places on the grid.

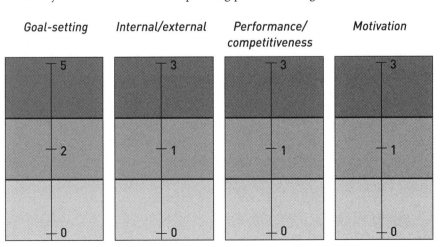

Goal-setting	Internal/external	Performance/ competitiveness	Motivation
5 / 2 / 0	3 / 1 / 0	3 / 1 / 0	3 / 1 / 0

Analysis of results and ideas for your development

The goal-setting questionnaire is divided into and looks at four elements of goal-setting.

1. Goal-setting itself – do you have a tendency to set goals or not?

2. Internal and external reference – do you tend to set your own goals or do you prefer to have others set them for you?

3. Performance or competitiveness – do you set personal performance goals or do you strive to achieve more competitive goals e.g. to be the top performer, to be in the highest percentage etc?

4. Motivation – how do you drive yourself to achieve goals? Does recognition and reward motivate you or do you tend to be motivated by what will happen if you don't achieve you goals?

Although the questionnaire has been divided into four parts it is important that you view the results as a whole as well as the individual parts. Remember the questionnaire is a guide for you to think about how you go about setting (or not) your goals and objectives. It is not designed to label you as a particular type of person but more to offer feedback and thoughts you may want to consider when you need to set goals and objectives.

Goal-setting

High score (35+) indicates that you already have a tendency to think through and set clear goals and outcomes. You may want to ask yourself whether you consistently think through and set clear directions for every one of your goals or whether you sometimes have a tendency to just think through the more important or more attractive goals. Consider also how the different goals and objectives you have impact on one another. That said, this a positive score – keep up the good work.

Medium score (15–34) indicates that although you might have the skills and knowledge to set clear goals and outcomes and achieve what you set out to you don't always set a clear direction and plan for yourself. The consequence of approaching situations without a clear direction is that on occasion you might find yourself unprepared for certain responses or results you get and then find yourself having to 'go back to the drawing board'. A few extra moments' investment in clearly thinking through your goals would be beneficial to you. Think about situations where you do construct well-formed goals and use the skills you already have to apply to other goals and outcomes you want to achieve.

Low score (0–14) indicates that you very rarely set goals of any sort. You run the risk of being heavily influenced by circumstances and others around you rather than being in control. You may well have successes although they could well be just a result of situations you've fallen upon or you just happened to be in the right place at the right time. There is a strong recommendation that you think about the benefits of setting yourself clear goals, maybe just one or two to begin with, so that you can begin to train yourself to think in this particular way. You may want to ask a colleague, coach or someone you trust to help you.

Internal/external

High score (25+) indicates that you have a strong preference for setting your own goals. In principle this is a very strong trait as it means that as you set your own goals you also 'own' them, making it potentially more likely that you will achieve success. You may want to bear in mind that 'sanity checking' your goals and objectives with someone else might be useful particularly if you work in a team environment where a common approach is needed. Checking your goals with a manager or colleague will also give you the opportunity to measure the goals you set. For instance, by setting yourself goals that are very difficult to achieve you may stand the risk of becoming disappointed or frustrated.

Medium score (12–24) indicates that you possibly prefer a 'negotiated' style of goal-setting. This could be where both you and a manager agree goals. This appears again to be a very positive way of setting goals. Be aware that you'll need to be remain assertive and challenging, not only to the person that you are setting goals with but also to yourself.

Low score (0–11) indicates that you prefer to have your goals set for you by someone else. Although there is no apparent harm in this preference you may want to ask yourself how motivated you really are by this way of goal-setting. Some people prefer this style because if they then fail to achieve the objective there is the opportunity to blame the person who set the goal (it was too high, too much etc.). There is a strong recommendation that you play a greater part in setting the goals that you need to achieve.

Performance/competitiveness

High score (25+) indicates that you have a strong preference for creating performance related goals. A performance-related goal is a goal the result of which is completely under your own control. For example, you may set a goal for completing a project by a certain time and date as opposed to being one of the first to finish. The person who creates performance-related goals can sometimes become frustrated if the goals they achieve still leave them behind colleagues and so it's important that the goals set are sanity-checked with a colleague or manager.

Medium score (12–24) indicates that you can create performance-related and competitive goals. A performance-related goal is where your own performance and behaviour is the primary influence on the outcome. For example, you might set a goal to see a certain amount of customers in a day. A competitive goal is one where you have no real way of knowing whether you can achieve your goal or not as the outcome is dependent on others. An example of a competitive goal is 'to be in the top 10 per cent of performers'. In this example you are dependent on 90 per cent of people not doing as well as you do. Unless you can predict the performance of others your competitive goal may not be that well thought out. The message is simple. By all means create goals that are performance- and competitiveness-related providing you have the necessary evidence to hand (i.e. what others will be doing). If you don't have the evidence then concentrate on your own performance.

Low score (0–11) indicates your preference for setting competitive goals (for example, to be number one, to be in the top ten) and although there's nothing wrong with this approach to setting goals, here is a word of caution. If you set purely competitive goals then you have little control over whether you achieve them or not because you are reliant on someone else or on another person's performance. For instance, if your goal is to be in the top three performers out of a group of 20, your goal then becomes dependent on 17 other people – over whom you have no control – performing less well than you. The only way to overcome this situation is to gain some credible evidence of what other people are capable of (usually based on past performance) and then to set your own performance goal that achieves more than the other person is capable of.

You are urged to consider this when you construct your goals and objectives.

Motivation

High score (22+) indicates a high preference for reward and recognition and that you often build these preferences into your goals. Nearly every well-formed goal and objective has a motivator attached to it and a pleasurable and healthy motivator is considered to be the most beneficial. Make sure that you continue to build these motivators into your goals. If there is any word of caution we can offer it would be to keep your goals realistic so that your motivator is achieved more often than not, otherwise disappointment could be a result.

Medium score (11–21) indicates that you are sometimes motivated by pleasurable reward and at other times by the risk of rebuke or pain if you don't perform. You may want to consider which you prefer and whether there is a link with who sets the goal. For instance, are you more motivated to be rewarded if you set your own goal and more motivated by pain if someone else sets your goals?

Low score (0–10) indicates that you are primarily motivated by what will happen if you don't perform or that you don't consider rewards that important. Either way, please consider your own values or what you stand to achieve if you reach your goals and objectives and look to replace pain with something more pleasurable.

Chapter 5 Creating a well-formed sales goal
(Getting ready)

SMART objectives (**S**pecific **M**easured **A**ction-based **R**ealistic **T**imed) only serve to give you an idea of what you want to achieve. A well-formed goal also needs to have the *how?* incorporated into it, so consider the following questions:

- What do I want to achieve?

- How will I know I have been successful?

- What will I be doing to move the sales process forward (using the Effective Selling Principles of this book)?

- What will be my fallback goal if for some reason I don't achieve my main sales goal?

- What have I learnt about the way I create sales goals and what will I do with the feedback from the goal-setting questionnaire?

Feel free to use the following sales goal promp sheet to help you create your sales goals.

CREATING A WELL-FORMED SALES GOAL

'Getting ready'

WHAT DO I WANT TO ACHIEVE ?

HOW WILL I DEMONSTRATE LIKING, LISTENING, AND UNDERSTANDING ?

WHAT PRODUCTIVE QUESTIONS SHOULD I ASK ?

WHAT WILL I NEED TO PRESENT MY PRODUCT / SERVICE SOLUTION ?

HOW WILL I GET A COMMITMENT TO ACTION THAT IS OWNED, ACTIVE AND PUBLIC ?

**Creating a well-formed
sales goal**
Get ready!

**Gaining a
commitment
to action**
Sold!

Effective
selling
programme

**Creating and
maintaining a
valuable
customer
relationship**
Liking and
listening

**Providing
what
is valuable to
the customer**
Giving 'em what they want

**Establishing
what is valuable
to the customer**
Being productive

Sold!

(Effective selling in action)

The essence of the Effective Selling Principles that we have described to you in this book are based on a set of well-researched and proven principles that actually work. We have maintained throughout that the intent of our book and the Effective Selling Principles it describes is to make the sales process less complex and complicated than it can often appear to be.

There are many thousands of tips and techniques in many hundreds of books that promise the best way to selling and we're recommending that you discard many of these in favour of the handful of trusted and proven principles we offer.

Your life as a sales person is complex enough without added complications and more techniques and sales strategies to think about. In a way, having more to think about could actually make you less effective because your attention is diverted away from the customer and is focused internally on what you need to do to sell and not what you need do to help the customer to buy from you. Hopefully the Effective Selling Principles will direct your attention to a handful of critical elements that will make the difference. In a way we're not only making it easy for people to buy from you, we're also making it easier for you to sell to those people.

But, in reality, how easy is it?

While we've provided you with what on the face of it is an easy and straightforward set of principles, the hard bit has now arrived. And that's to incorporate these tools so that they become part of your everyday selling job, and that's going to require some investment and practice on your part. What we can do in order to help you is to look at some common sales scenarios and situations that you could well find yourself in and talk about how the five Effective Selling Principles can be applied to such situations and scenarios. In order for us to do this we asked a number of sales professionals to review the principles we have presented in this book and talk to us about situations they find themselves in on a day-to-day basis. The result was a set of questions, which we are going to take in turn and answer by applying the principles described in this book. Hopefully this will help you to incorporate the things you have taken in and give you ideas for using them yourself to make you a more successful sales professional.

The principles you describe seem too simple. Is that really it?

Yes, they are simple but that's not the whole story. The hard part is taking the time to understand and use these principles so that they become part of your day-to-day sales activities. And that requires an investment of time and practice on your part – and not just any practice. 'Practice makes perfect' as the saying goes, although that's not quite strictly the case. You can practise things badly and all that will happen is that you will get good at doing things badly. As Vinci Lombardi, the hugely successful American NFL coach pointed out – 'perfect practice makes perfect'. Focusing on what works and what skills and behaviours you use that generate success makes for more meaningful and useful results. And it's here that we recommend that you ask for some help. You know when you've been successful – the signs are there for all to see. A delighted customer, a sales presentation you've made that leaves the audience fully convinced and ready for action. In order to recreate that success you need a way of knowing what has caused your success. But how can you witness your own performance and provide an honest and accurate reflection of how you used the Effective Selling Principles to achieve that success? In order to understand where your strengths and weakness lie and to be able to practise those skills perfectly you need a little help from someone else. We suggest that you ask a colleague or your manager to accompany you on a few sales calls you make to customers and give you some feedback about how you are doing. It might be a cliché but the words in this book will always be just words in a book unless you make them mean something to you by trying these principles out and practising them perfectly.

Can you give an example of all the principles in action in a sales call?

Let's assume that you're a sales representative for a stationary supplier and you're going to visit a retailer who has five stores on your territory for the first time. Let's take the five principles in turn and apply them to this sales call.

Firstly, you need to *create a well-formed sales goal* by asking yourself what you want to achieve by visiting this customer. If you're currently not supplying to this potential customer maybe your sales goal is to take a new order. If the customer already buys from your company your sales goal might be to sell a particular new product or maybe to increase this customer's usual monthly order. The key to a well-formed sales goal is that the result you want is a sale or a commitment that moves the sale forward in a productive way. Let's assume that your sales goal is to get the customer to purchase a case of paper products from a new range your company has launched. Now that you have a sales goal you simply need to review how you will use the other four Effective Selling Principles to achieve your goal. The next thing you should do is think about and plan to establish and maintain a valuable relationship with the customer. You do this by *liking and listening*. What do you know already about this customer that you can use to show that you share similarities with them? What genuine compliments can you pay and where can you show that you can work co-operatively with them. Remember that when you're having a discussion with the customer you should repeat back their words to demonstrate your understanding of what they are saying to you. After giving some thought to how you're going to create and maintain a valuable relationship through the use of listening and liking you should now turn your attention to what questions you will ask. Think through in advance of the sales call the types of productive questions that you can ask the customer that get to the heart of what they're wanting and that will also move you towards your sales goal. Also think about some related information that you could share with the customer during the questioning stage so that the conversation is not too one-sided or interrogational. Following on from the productive questioning stage, you will need to consider the ways that you'll present your product and proposal to the customer. Remember, they may wish to see some examples or look at specific information, they may want to discuss certain elements of your proposals or might even want to try out a sample of the new range. You should ensure that you have everything to hand and available. At this stage you should also give consideration to a small drawback or weakness that you can reveal to the customer that will make your subsequent presentation more credible and impactful. Finally, what sort of commitment will you need from the customer? Clearly the best outcome is a signed order but what if during the sales interaction you find that other people are involved in the decision? What active and public commitments that are owned by your customer would be most likely to move the sale forward? Can you speak to other people involved in the decision today or will the customer be willing to arrange for you to see them at another time?

> **The key to a well-formed sales goal is that the result you want is a sale or a commitment that moves the sale forward in a productive way.**

By taking each principle of effective selling in turn and thinking through in advance you can see how simple and straightforward the sales process can be. It also gives you a very clear vision of what you will be doing, so when you actually come to make the sales call it's almost like you are doing it for the second time – and generally we all find something easier the second time we do it. In the appendix we have included a sales goal prompter for you to use if you wish.

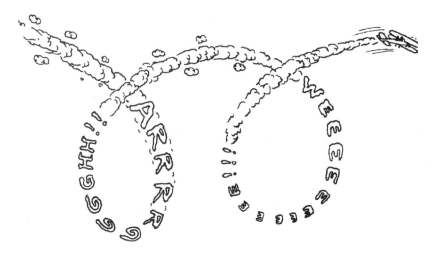

'It's easier to do things for the second time'

I've used a number of different selling techniques in the past. Surely selling is selling. What is so different about the Effective Selling Principles and *Sold!*?

We agree that selling is selling and, apart from a few changes in the words used to describe what you as a sales person are doing, the fundamentals are very similar to other sales processes and models you may have encountered in the past. There are, however, two things that are different about the Effective Selling Principles. The first is the whole idea that rather than selling to people you're there to help them to buy from you, therefore the agenda of the sales call is focused on what you can do for the customer not the other way round. The second difference is in how you apply the Effective Selling Principles and it's here that the simple approach becomes most useful. The Effective Selling Principles focus your mind and attention on the handful of ways that'll make it easier for people to buy from you. You can have every complex and advanced trick in the book but if you haven't got these fundamentals right then your sales success will be affected. Think about all the different top performers like sports people, television presenters and even the celebrity chefs. They are at the peak of their performance because they practise the fundamentals. They consistently focus on the handful of basic skills that lead to their success. Footballers practise passing the ball. Runners work on how to get out of the starting blocks in the quickest time. Television presenters focus on how to clearly and concisely communicate a message or story. In the case of the celebrity chefs, they all have a basic set of tools and skills from which they create their recipes. Sure, they may use spices and seasoning to enhance the dish and create recipes but they also know that too much spice can spoil the dish. The same is true of effective selling. Get the fundamental principles right because without them no amount of spice and seasoning will rescue the sale.

What evidence is there that these principles work?

All the principles we have presented in this book have been tried and tested in both a research format and with real sales teams selling to real customers every single day. They have worked in business-to-business scenarios, field sales, fast-moving consumer goods environments, healthcare and pharmaceutical selling, retailing and even on the petrol forecourts.[1] We're not going to make huge claims that using these principles will increase your sales by 400 per cent overnight because they won't. What we can show, though, is that skilfully using the principles described in this book will give you incrementally increased sales revenues. In addition to the obvious sales measures there's also a sales profiling tool that you can use to evaluate your own sales skills against the Effective Selling Principles. You can download this tool free of charge from www.business-minds.com

> **Get the fundamental principles right because without them no amount of spice and seasoning will rescue the sale.**

How do the principles in this book apply to 'bigger ticket' sales?

The amount or value of the sale is important and will often create a degree of complexity with perhaps more people being involved in the decision-making process or perhaps the production of lengthy proposals and some-

---

1. Absolutely true. One garage wanted to increase the number of repeat customers as most of their business was passing trade. Using the Effective Selling Principles they were able to increase the number of returning customers and hence their sales revenues.

times tendering. The fact is, though, that the principles hold true in the sales interactions themselves. Whether you are writing a proposal, making a presentation to the board of a company or doing any other activity related to a high-value sale, the fundamental skills that you're using will be identical and therefore the Effective Selling Principles apply. Athletes don't change their basic skills when they compete in crucial events. They use the same set of skills they would if they were running at their practice track. The principles we've discussed have been used to successfully help customers buy products ranging from a few pence to hundreds of thousands of pounds.

The fact is that most customers complain about the price and say that my product is too expensive. How can I deal with this?

We won't bore you with how much money we would have if someone gave us a pound everytime we heard this. Better to actually offer some practical advice on how to deal with this situation. One thing that you need to know if a customer thinks your product is expensive is what they're comparing it to. We can present a product that costs £25 and make it appear either expensive or cheap depending on what we compare it to. Compared to a product of £5 it's five times more expensive yet compared to one that is £50 our product represents a big saving. If you believe price is going to be an issue then think back to the principle of providing what is valuable to the customer and the idea of admitting a weakness or drawback to your product before you present your proposal. It's here that you should place a message about the cost of your product or service and you should deliver that message by comparing it to other options the customer could consider that makes your product appear less expensive. The key to this is in the timing. If you wait for the customer to say that's too expensive then they have their own comparison in their mind; this could be more difficult to deal with, as it becomes an owned opinion that they have. It's a good idea to compare your product's price with common competitors and come up with some ideas that you can use to present your product in a better light. For example, everyone knows that Fairy Liquid is more expensive than some other brands but it also lasts longer. By comparing Fairy Liquid in this way it can be presented as being more cost-effective than cheaper brands as you get more liquid for your money. Remember though you can have the best argument in the world, but if you present it at the wrong time it gets lost. The key is to know the best time to make your case. The timing is essential or you could just end up have an argument about price, which is unproductive for both you and the customer.[1]

What about dealing with the difficult customer? What can I do to get the awkward customer back on my side?

Surprisingly the first thing you should do is relatively simple and straightforward and yet it's often very easy to forget to do it. Imagine that you're in a sales call with a customer. Things seem to be going well – in fact you are on a roll. Then suddenly it happens. The customer comes up with a comment or question that throws you completely off balance. It may be an objection or maybe the customer has an opinion that's different to yours. In some cases they are just being awkward for the sake of being awkward. Whatever the disagreement or hostility is, you need to deal with the situation you are faced with.

The most natural reaction is to immediately defend your position. There is a variety of ways you can do this. You might have a standard response to an objection, you might rebut their argument with your argument, you might present a piece of data that disproves their particular point of view. However, as well as considering what your response should be you might also want to think about the timing of your response.

By immediately defending your position or proposition you run the risk of sending a message to the customer that you haven't heard them or, even worse, that they're wrong. The customer will naturally now defend their position even more and will in all probability become more committed to it. This will make your job of helping them to buy from you even more difficult. Whilst it's important to get your message across or to correct a misunderstanding, the timing of it can make all the difference.

Roger Fisher is one of the world's most respected negotiation lecturers at Harvard Business School. He makes the point that when two people are in disagreement the first thing they should do is to attempt to find an area

---

1. The alternative answer to this question is that your product *is* just too expensive. Common symptoms include customers screwing up their faces, pulling their hair out and screaming 'How %^!*ing much?'

where they can agree. People who can agree are potentially more likely to listen to one another's point of view. So in these situations before you begin to respond to their objection or counter their argument you need to get them agreeing with you. The easiest way to do this is to simply use the 'parrotphrasing' tool and repeat back what the customer said to you *before* you respond to their objection or problem.

A good way to do this is to say: 'So let me make sure I understand you. You think . . . *[insert exactly what they said]* . . . Is that right?' To which the customer must answer 'Yes'.

At least the customer is now in some form of agreement with you and you've also sent the message that you've listened to them and understood them. This will make it more likely that the next thing you say will have a greater chance of being considered; this should be a productive question that gets to the heart of their difficulty or objection.

A simple thing we know, and used in a calm and deliberate manner can have great results for you. It is just amazing the number of sales people that do the alternative and get defensive.

One of the most frustrating tasks a sales person has is to try and generate leads from new customers and this often means calling them on the telephone. How can the Effective Selling Principles be used in situations such as these?

We're often asked this question and we realize it can be a daunting task for many sales people. Often referred to as 'cold calling' it involves picking up the telephone to potential customers that may or may not have an interest in your product and generating an appointment to go and see them or a even a sale. Herein lies the first clue about how to approach this task. You need to be clear about what sort of customer is most likely to be a potential customer. In the Introduction we spoke of the different types of companies in terms of whether they are Price, Product or Service Leading Companies. It's important that you understand what your company offering is and then ensure that the customers that you call first are the sort that will appreciate your offering. Once you have established such a list you are then in a position to make contact and for this you'll need a well-formed sales goal. What do you want to achieve? An appointment? An order?

SOLD

A sale? Once you have a sales goal firmly fixed in your mind you need to have an opening statement that will capture the potential customer's attention and show how your company can help them. Using the listening and liking principle and then asking a productive question is an effective way to do this. For example: *'Hello, my name is Sue and I am calling from [name of company]. We are an experienced supplier of [product] to companies that are similar to yours and we would very much like the opportunity to supply you with [product]. How could we make this possible?'*

You need to be clear about what sort of customer is most likely to be a potential customer.

One potential response to this approach could be 'no thanks' in which case you would thank the person for their time and politely enquire if you might call them again in a few months time to see if their needs have changed. On the other hand, they may express an interest and you are off and running. You're now in a position to establish what is valuable to the customer, provide it and get a commitment to action, which could be an order or an appointment to go and see the customer.

What if they just ask you to just send some more information or a brochure though?

Some people just don't like saying no to others and might use the 'could you send me some more information' tactic to avoid telling the sales person that they're really not interested. At other times they might genuinely want more information in order to make a decision about whether to talk more with you. One thing is certain. You and your company don't want to waste money sending out expensive brochures any more than the recipient wants to spend their time opening them and then throwing them in the bin – and that's just the start. Having sent out information to a potential customer you will probably contact them again by telephone to check they have received it and try and take the sales process forward (exactly what the customer wants to avoid). Better then to be up front and honest with the customer and ask for an owned and active commitment from them before you send any further information to them.

'I know that some people ask me to send information to them even though they have no genuine interest in me and my company. If that's the case then I don't mind you telling me, as I don't want to keep contacting you and wasting your time. However, if you do genuinely want some more information perhaps you could tell me a little more about what you might be looking for and then I can be sure to send you exactly the sort of information you are looking for. You may even prefer me to come and speak with you directly.'

This approach, whilst direct, does get to the heart of what's valuable to the customer and can eliminate wasted time and money from both yours and the customer's perspective. We're not advocating being bolshy or rude, just being realistic. It might need a little bravery on your part to begin with but it can be a highly effective way of generating an initial commitment from your potential customer very early on.

What have the Effective Selling Principles got in common with key account management and can they be applied to managing major accounts and customers?

Key account management and selling are two different things although there's often confusion due to the overlap of common skills that are required to do both. In true key account management the person managing the account or 'customer' is in a role of managing the whole interface between the supplier and the customer. Other definitions we've seen are focused on selling in key accounts, which is different to key account management. The skills and principles described in this book, however, are common skills that can be used in a number of situations. The ability to plan effectively, create and maintain relationships and have productive interactions that focus on the benefit of the supplier and the customer are clearly required and therefore the principles are transferable. One thing that's worthy of mention is knowing which of your customers gives you the most business and which customers represent the best potential. Often referred to as 'adoption ladders' these are systems to classify your customers and help you to get an overall picture of how your customers compare against everyone else. For example, a 'gold' customer could be one that represents big business opportunities and use of your products and services on a preferred basis. A 'silver' customer could be a regular purchaser of your products but might also purchase other suppliers' products. Similarly, a 'bronze' customer could be a less regular purchaser and so on and so on. The focus is then on how to get more 'bronze' customers to become 'silver', 'silver' to 'gold' and the like.[1]

What can I do to evaluate myself against the principles and get an idea of how well I am doing?

Visit www.business-minds.com and download the Effective Selling Programme Evaluation Tool. It will ask you to rate yourself against 50 selling situations and will then provide an overview of your sales skills and current performance. Also included on this site are some ideas about how you can develop your skills further.

We are more than happy to answer any further questions and would be delighted to hear your comments. You can e-mail us direct at sold@salesinteraction.com

Good luck and remember:

In order to be number one – practise like you are number two.

---

1. We are happy to offer you, free of charge, our own customer classification system that goes like this: platypus, stork, heron, duck, budgie (it's all about how big the bills we send them are!).